The MANY FACES *of* HAPPINESS

Inspiring Stories on What Makes People Happy

Elisabeth Oosterhoff

THE MANY FACES OF HAPPINESS
Inspiring Stories on What
Makes People Happy

Copyright © 2019 by Elisabeth Oosterhoff

ISBN: 978-0-578-57362-5
Printed in the United States of America

The views expressed herein are those of the author and do not necessarily reflect the views of the United Nations.

Published by Elisabeth Oosterhoff

Cover Design: Eric Labacz, www.labaczdesign.com

To Nama

Table of Contents

Introduction

It was 2 p.m. on 31 December, and the growing excitement was palpable in the hallways of the United Nations Headquarters in New York City, where its staff members eagerly awaited an announcement for early release. I was chatting with Alejandro, a messenger from Colombia, about New Year's resolutions when the idea of interviewing one person about happiness each day for an entire year struck me like lightning.

Like one of my dear primary school teachers always said, "Once Elisabeth gets an idea in her head, it's very difficult to change her mind." The following day marked the beginning of a wonderful, enlightening adventure, in which I interviewed 365 people whom I affectionately called my "happiness dates." My interviews mostly took place in the United States but some were in Japan and Spain.

My "happiness dates" came from all walks of life. I strove to encompass the widest possible spectrum and wanted to gain insight from different socio-economic, religious, cultural, gender, and age perspectives. A five-year-old Haitian boy was the youngest person interviewed, and my 98-year-old neighbor was the oldest. I conducted interviews on the streets, by the river, on trains, on planes, in cafes, in stores, in restaurants…you name it!

The more people I encountered, the more fascinated I became to discover their hopes, dreams, and sometimes regrets but with an overall goal of bringing forth what made them happy.

You may wonder if total strangers are willing to share their innermost thoughts on what might appear as a very personal subject. To this I will reply that about 95 per cent of those I approached generously agreed to be interviewed but there was obviously a cautious effort to choose prospective subjects who seemed more receptive and open. I sincerely believe that most of us enjoy when somebody takes a genuine interest in us, when we feel understood, and our voice is truly heard.

It was not always easy to be "the happiness lady" but it was necessary to project a happy face when I went searching for my "happiness dates." I would say, "I am putting on my happiness hat," and off I went. I occasionally felt that I nourished myself from others' happiness.

There were, of course, also rejections, and on some days one rejection would be followed by another and another. Maybe in these instances, despite my efforts, I did not project enough positive energy.

A few times I reached out to prospects who appeared sad, hoping that my request to make them search for happiness within would give them, at least temporarily, some relief and a happier mood. My altruistic intentions were not always appreciated when people just wanted to be left alone—especially when all they wanted was to sleep on the train. Apart from these instances, our conversations were like a wonderful dance: Just as they shared and confided in me, I shared in return, as I did not want only to "take." It was not unusual for tears to be shed.

It was difficult to select the interviews to include in this book because, to me, they were all special. However, I had to extract what, in my opinion, seemed the most striking facets of our conversations.

Although the causes for happiness varied from person to person, from generation to generation, some of the most common factors were family, friends, helping others, travelling, enjoying food and drinks, being active, being creative, nature, art, faith, and music. Only a couple of people mentioned money, and even fewer said their job brought them joy. There were more women than men whose jobs made them happy.

It was especially their stories that made an impact on me, such as confessions about first kisses, tiring but rewarding fishing trips, train voyages in India, the fall of Communism, miracles, declarations of love after 60 years of marriage, a soldier's return from Iraq, and many more.

The interviews were not always about being happy but also about sorrow, as without sadness we wouldn't know what happiness is. Some of these were the man who lost his son, the lady who found her husband in bed with his lover after 20 years of marriage, the lady who became homeless after losing her job, and the mom who couldn't identify any causes for happiness because her son was a heroin addict and her family life was collapsing.

These interviews illustrate that no matter where you come from, what religion you are, your sexual orientation, or the color of your skin, we all strive for happiness, and we are all worthy of it. Instead of nurturing prejudices and intolerance, let us instead embrace our differences, get inspired from each other, and create a better and happier world. This will only come from listening to and learning from our fellow citizens.

I hope that my readers will find inspiration in these stories, people they can identify with, and know that they are not alone. Most of all I wish that this book will bring as much happiness and encouragement to you readers as it has brought to me.

My dear "happiness dates," I am eternally grateful to all of you whom I encountered on my path; you took the time to speak with me and entrusted me with your thoughts and stories. You taught me much, reminded me to be appreciative for all things small and big, to be brave in the midst of adversities, and most importantly, that happiness is a choice. I think of you often: You keep inspiring me to be a better person. Thank you! It makes me happy to think that, with this book, your wisdom, humor, and joy will be brought forth to many more!

Elisabeth Oosterhoff

Gross National Happiness

About a month ago I typed in the word "happiness" on my Facebook account. A few references showed up but there was particularly one that captured my attention: *Gross National Happiness: 68 Miles from Thimphu,* a documentary from Bhutan, where Karen, the producer, had asked its inhabitants what made them happy. It was exactly what I had done here, thousands of miles away!

The term "gross national happiness" appeared in 1972 when a journalist had asked the then King of Bhutan, Jigme Singye Wangchuck, what the gross national product (GNP) of his country was, to which the King is reported to have replied, "I am not interested in the gross national product but in the gross national happiness (GNH) of my people." A sophisticated survey was created to measure the population's quality of life, spanning from wealth and employment, physical and mental health, recreation, education, leisure time to the environment. Before policies are implemented in Bhutan, they are submitted to a GNH survey. In the 2005 Population and Housing Census in Bhutan, question number 13 was: "Are you happy?"

I sent Karen an email explaining the nature of my project and asked to interview her. A month went by without news.

One day my cell phone rings. "Hi, this is Karen. You wrote me an email a while ago but I was out of the country travelling. I am back and would love to meet you!"

I am ecstatic. Our meeting place is a restaurant in Lambertville, New Jersey, an artsy hamlet sitting on the bank of the Delaware River. It is a warm day, and we sit down in the patio.

"How did you get the idea to do this documentary, Karen?"

"The idea of a country that had this concept of gross national happiness as the bedrock of how they want to govern really appealed to me, and also the executive producer of our film had a deep fascination with Bhutan. We travelled there in October 2006 and stayed until January 2007, and I went back the following year to observe and film their first democratic election in March 2008, after the King had voluntarily stepped down.

"In Bhutan most people live in rural areas—some of them had to walk three days to a voting station and still there was this amazing turnout, over 80 per cent. Although the King of Bhutan had announced a decade ago that he would do this, it was almost unimaginable, after 400 years of monarchy. The King is so beloved that for the most part, people didn't want it. Every single person has a picture of the King on their walls. There is a real reverence for him. It was extremely emotional for people when he stepped down.

"I remember reading the coronation speech of the new King on 7 November, and being very moved by his words: 'As long as we continue to pursue the simple and timeless goal of being good human beings, and as long as we strive to build a nation that stands for everything that is good….As citizens of a spiritual land, you treasure the qualities of a good human being: honesty, kindness, charity, integrity, unity, respect for our culture and traditions, love for our country and for God.'"

"Why did you call your movie *Gross National Happiness: 68 Miles from Thimphu?*"

"The radius we travelled was approximately 68 miles out of Thimphu. Many places in Bhutan, especially the eastern part, are very isolated and hard to get to. Just in that radius, travelling back and forth among the different characters was hard. We just saw a fraction of what Bhutan really was."

"Did you think a lot about happiness before making this documentary?"

"I guess everybody tries to figure out what makes them happy. When I was young, we travelled a lot with my father, who was a psychiatrist and interested in other people and cultures. In Europe and the Middle East, I discovered different ways of how people celebrate weddings, deal with death, express their spirituality. Going to Bhutan heightened that experience because their approach and perception of happiness and contentment shape their culture. The most important factor is the value of community. So much of what I enjoyed was just sitting in a place, socializing, and meeting people.

"In Bhutan, most people still live in agrarian communities. They still depend on each other, sharing tools; their families have grown up in the same area. It is rapidly changing because people are now migrating to the capital city, Thimphu. Schoolchildren often have to walk one or two hours to their local school. At the time of the day when school starts and ends, it's very common to just pick up some children and drive them the rest of the way home. Those practices make the country feel very comforting and familial. If you have relatives that live in the countryside and you live in the city, they will come and visit you and fully expect to stay with you for a certain period of time. There are some levels of family obligations that might not be as easy as you want but they still exist, and because of this, I think people are much more tolerant. You cannot just live in your house behind a fence and not interact with other people in your community."

"Apart from the strong sense of community, what can the West learn in terms of happiness from Bhutan? What's their secret?"

"A lot of people have asked me this question," she reflects before continuing. "We cannot all go and live in Bhutan, breathe fresh air, and farm. In Bhutan, they practice Mahayana Buddhism, which promotes the idea that practitioners should not just seek personal enlightenment but the enlightenment of all beings. In the Bhutanese society, the culture is geared toward seeking to raise the consciousness of everyone else, of other beings in the world. I think it goes back to the fact that too much emphasis on self, on unending desire, causes a lot of suffering and unhappiness. People often say that some of the keys to being happy are to be of service to others, to shift the focus off yourself and onto others. Being in Bhutan emphasized that point. Then again, it's changing, more modern culture and more modern self-awareness. It's just the way the world is evolving, and we cannot do anything about it.

"The first time I visited Bhutan, I was doing a location scout. We were hiking somewhere not that far away. The guide said, 'I would like to see if we can walk to this farmhouse where some friends of mine, an old Tibetan couple, live. We will see if they are home.' So we are at the van, and we are just going to walk for half an hour or 45 minutes. I have my video camera, my film camera, lenses, raincoat, jacket, and all I am thinking about is: 'Is it going to rain? Am I going to be hot, cold, wet?' Ten minutes of this! I end up walking from the van with all this junk hanging off me because the fear of being uncomfortable was so strong. All I could think about was the thought of not getting what I came to get. I was so lost in that. We walked past some monks who had probably been walking for hours from the monastery to the marketplace with one pair of shoes and what I came to refer to as 'a monk bag,' which is a cloth bag about 12 by 18 inches. At the end of the trip I was thinking, 'If I couldn't fit my stuff in a monk bag, then it wouldn't come with me.' I just became more and more aware of how weighted down I was, so heavy with all my things, expectations, and all my worry about my stuff.

"We finally arrived at a beautiful old farmhouse and met a couple in their 80s. We went inside. They were so gracious. A group of six people just turned up from nowhere interrupting their day to serve us tea. We sat there and chatted with them. In Bhutan in the countryside, people don't have furniture: They sit on a mat on the floor and sleep on a mat that gets rolled out at night. They will have an altar, and that's basically it. It might be one room with a kitchen in the back. In my mind, I was thinking, 'This couple has been married for 50 years so where is all their stuff?' There was a photograph of the Dalai Lama and some other religious figures by their altar. The man was a metalsmith; he made bowls and ladles and utilitarian things of that sort so those were hanging on the walls. They did not have more than they needed. They had a farm and plenty to eat. I asked them, 'What would make you happy? What, other than what you have, would you like?' They answered, 'It would be nice for us to have a road that is closer to the house: It would make it easier to get to the market. But you know what, our kids are educated and have their own lives now so we would like to move closer to a monastery.' In Bhutan, it is a very auspicious thing in your later life to live close to a monastery. That was kind of it! Before leaving their house, I took a picture of it because I wanted to remember this feeling and the vision of living only with what one needed.

"When I came back to the States, it was Christmastime, and I went to a mall where I was overwhelmed by what I saw. I noticed a completely functionless ornate table that you couldn't really use as a table; on top of it was a bowl that you couldn't eat from or wash. Inside the bowl were decorative balls that didn't mean anything. They were just balls. The whole thing probably cost about $400. I remember thinking, 'How could you explain a thing like this to this couple in Bhutan? How would you even explain that in the West we would pay $400 for these completely useless balls in a useless bowl on a useless table?' When I came back from my second trip to Bhutan that spring, I had a huge garage sale and got rid of a lot of things. I am not saying that I am a person without stuff. I was just sickened by the amount of unnecessary things I had.

"I also think they had clearly defined life goals. They didn't have these unending climbing-the-corporate-ladder goals but were just more in touch with the finite sets of goals that they wanted to attain to make them happy.

"A lot of people might go to Bhutan thinking they will find happiness there, that they will stumble around, walk into a monastery, a light will shine on them, and that their lives will change. It was a very magical and spiritual place for me. Oh my God, there are monks all over the place! I came back and was taken in by the optics of what

I thought that meant, the sight of so many monks in robes walking about. I didn't understand it at all.

"Each time I went to Bhutan, I understood it more clearly, and my wish, my belief, that it was some kind of Shangri-La would be challenged by the reality of what I witnessed there. At first, I was quite depressed to discover that this was not Shangri-La. Bhutanese people are just people, who like us, wrestle with greed, corruption, and drug abuse. I found out there are monks everywhere but, in fact, they are not all scholarly monks who feel a calling to gain spiritual knowledge. There are many lay monks for whom it is a job to perform prayers and rituals. As I learnt more about the reality of the culture, it kind of came full circle, and I understood there is actually something quite lovely about the idea that we are really all exactly the same everywhere. To think that there is a place where people are unaffected by the downfalls of human nature is an unrealistic ideal. That realization is depressing at first but when that breaks down, you acknowledge that they are exposed to the same things that we are."

"Do you think they are happier than we are?" I interject.

"I think that they are happier because in many ways life is simpler for many people, and I believe that many of us would be happier if we had a simpler life and a stronger sense of community. Alienation and loneliness are major sources of unhappiness in Western culture."

"What questions did you ask them?"

"I would ask them about what were the happiest moments in their lives, what made them happy, what was missing in their lives, and if there was something that they would like, their hopes and dreams for themselves and their children, how they overcame problems, particularly things that had brought them a lot of sorrow. I especially asked this question to the women because it is a matriarchal society. They do the finances, and the property goes to the women."

"How do they overcome problems?"

"You don't complain about them, you just kind of get on with life. I remember one woman in particular. She was very religious and had yearned to be a nun; but she married and had a family so she couldn't pursue that goal any longer. It was a painful loss. For her, it was about duty and religion but she would pray every day. Every morning she would come out and perform certain rituals.

"What is your definition of happiness, Karen?" I ask, and she pauses for a long time before answering.

"Happiness is feeling a sense of connectedness to what you do, and the people that you are with. If you can cultivate this in your life, it is a great source of happiness, and it gives you a feeling of accomplishment and contentment—much more than the realization of other ambitions that I had in my own career. I am so much happier now as I get older, when some of these ambitions dropped away. I don't feel 'I am not anyone until I have accomplished this or that thing.' Happiness will depend on how you spend most of the time of your life, and with whom you spend your time."

Silence comes over us. A plane passes in the sky.

"What were some of the happiest moments in your life, Karen?"

"One of the happiest moments in my life was when my now boyfriend came to visit me in Bhutan. We met online two weeks before I left the U.S. He came from England and flew into Philadelphia to visit me right before my trip. I was packing, getting ready to go, and was like "Whatever!" We spent one day together, and that was it. I told him I would be gone for a couple of months, which turned into three and a half months. We were online all the time and spoke on the phone. He decided to visit me in Bhutan. I don't think I had ever experienced that level of anticipation to see anybody in my life. Finally, he was there. They opened the doors, and he walked down the stairs, smiling. Not bad for a second date! Good effort! That was absolutely one of my happiest moments!

"The night we filmed a monk bathing in Bhutan was a very happy moment in my life. The monks do this thing called the hot stone bath: They walk into the woods, where they have tubs, and put hot stones in them. We hiked up to the baths with flashlights. I knew the monk we were filming but not that well. The act of him letting us watch him bathe—he wasn't naked or anything like that—was still such a private moment, and I felt so happy to be allowed to witness it. To be there with him and the other monks in the dark woods in the middle of nowhere, to hear the crackling of the logs, the click of the tong as they moved the coal, the smell of smoke as they were lighting the fire. When you looked up, there were tons of stars. He was reciting prayers as he was bathing. At nighttime you can let yourself feel that you disappear into that person. You know that he is not looking at you. For him, it was just a bath but for me, it was almost a religious and such a sensual experience. I will never forget that moment."

January

The day I see my wife again
Friday, 8 January

"What will make me very happy is when I see my wife again. You know she died, right?" My friend Wally, the train conductor, takes off his New Jersey Transit hat, wipes his forehead, and his eyes become watery. "She passed away many years ago from cancer. We went on 12 cruises together and used to get these nice cabins with a little balcony where we would sit and look at the sunset together. At the time, I was slim and handsome. I used to be in the Navy, and I travelled all over the place. We were very much in love."

Wally, train conductor

Paris

Monday, 11 January

This morning I interviewed my dear friend Danny during a phone call to Canada. She retired a few years ago and now takes care of her mother, who is in her 90s.

"I love to go on trips," she says. "Being Québécoise, I am very attached to Paris, and whenever I want a short escape, this is where I recharge my batteries. Even though I have found a wonderful care center for my mother, it's hard to travel for long periods of time because I feel that I am neglecting *Maman*.

"In the past when I visited Paris, I used to live in a *peniche* (houseboat) on the Seine, then later with some monks. Now I have found a small, reasonably priced hotel not far from the Champs-Élysées. So when the going gets tough, the snowfalls heavy, and I need some sunshine, I jump on a plane for a long weekend to Paris where I let Leonardo da Vinci, Rubens, Monet, Manet, Renoir, and Pissarro bring me back to life."

I can hear her smile as she remembers. "Every morning I take my coffee in a nice little café and my dinner at an intimate bistro. Sometimes, when I am really lucky, I even get to see Aznavour in a concert."

Small epiphanies in life
Tuesday, 12 January

My Sudanese friend Israa calls me in the office. After chatting for a while and exchanging good wishes for the year to come, I ask her to name three things that make her happy.

"To laugh until the belly hurts and you are gasping for air and can hardly talk, to love and be loved, and to have small epiphanies in life. To feel moments of connection, that life is perfect just the way it is. For instance, last Sunday when it had snowed—it didn't snow a lot but all the ground was covered. I had not really paid so much attention to it while I was inside but when I ventured outside and saw that everything was covered by this nice white layer, I became amazed at the beauty of nature."

Weekends

Friday, 15 January

I am dropping off my friend's son at a dance at his high school.
"What are three things that make you happy, Vicente?"
"To do sports, weekends, and summer."
Wise words from a 15-year-old boy!

My plants
Sunday, 24 January

Susan, one of my best friends, lives across the street from me. She inspires me and makes me want to grow and be a better human being. She is like a vitamin to me. I need a weekly dose, otherwise something is missing in my life.

"I have to go home soon but haven't interviewed anybody today. Would you mind telling me what makes you happy?" I ask.

She tilts her head with curiosity and says quickly, "Sure! My plants make me really happy." She points to a large dieffenbachia near the window and confidently pets the leaves of a money plant. "Since I am done having babies, the plants are my babies. I fall in love with them and enjoy seeing them grow. I think about them every day. This week all of them got topsoil. Plants are such a simple form to bring life into your life."

To pray
Tuesday, 26 January

At the end of a workshop on how to create a life map to reach our life goals, I interview one of my colleagues, Bibi, who is from Guinea.

"What makes you happy?"

"Helping others in small and big ways. They can be people I know or strangers. Ten years ago, I went on pilgrimage to Mecca; it changed my life. After this experience, I decided I wanted to dedicate my life to serving others. So I applied for my first mission assignment. I spent two years for the United Nations peace-keeping forces in East Timor and later in Darfur. Every day of those assignments I felt that my job was meaningful and wonderful. Today I dream of being part of a 'Quick Impact Mission' with the Department of Peace-Keeping Operations: We go to a location and, together with the local population, determine what their needs are, and then we implement it. Here you see results fast and efficiently.

"Praying makes me happy. I am a Muslim, and every morning, before the sun rises I do my morning prayer (*'fajr'*). Prayer relaxes me, makes me more serene, and helps me cope with whatever comes up during the course of the day."

Priesthood
Sunday, 31 January

I am circling the bookstore in search of a "happiness date." My eyes fall on an elderly gentleman with white hair, a navy-blue coat, and a plaid shirt who is sipping a cup of coffee.

"Excuse me, sir, may I ask you a question?"

"Sure," he says and points at the chair in front of him. "I am Father Ken, but you can call me Ken."

"Can you name a few things that make you happy, Father?"

A dreamy expression and a smile spread across his face.

"There are so many things that make me happy. The first thing is my priesthood. As a kid, I was a nominal Lutheran and not a churchgoer. But later on, when I went to college, I lived in a Polish neighborhood where there was a strong Catholic influence. In 1963, I converted to Catholicism, and after having lived a full life, I finally became a priest in 1987.

"However, priesthood is not only joy. It is difficult to be a priest sometimes. When you are alone, you can be lonely. Loneliness can lead to trouble. Today we see a lot of abuse within the Catholic Church, and I believe some of this stems from loneliness. But there is also a great beauty of being alone: It is a treasure chest, a place to cultivate the richness of being your own friend. Where do you discover God? Primarily in yourself. By cultivating your aloneness, you are communicating with God. There are a lot of ways of praying and of being close to God: I do this with great reading, beautiful music, and the arts. All these are places of great prayer.

"Heaven is not so much spatial; it is something that transpires in the human heart. 'God' means 'that which is other than me.' It can be that person over there, or you or her. Heaven is when you get to a point in your life when you have peace with yourself.

"As a priest, I do a lot of abstract thinking but the real world is not lived up there. My goal has been to take what's up there—spatial language—and to connect down here. In my job there has always been a tension between the abstract and the concrete thinking. My spiritual journey is to bring these together."

"How do you do this, Father Kenneth?"

"I have done a lot of teaching, I preach, and I talk with people. I believe that happiness is achieved to the extent that we can bring the abstract and the concrete together. Heart knowledge comes with age, not brain knowledge."

February

Sleeping
Monday, 1 February

I am still typing up the notes from the weekend when a well-dressed brunette sits down next to me on the train. She looks drained and somber. Although I don't really get the feeling that she is an extrovert, I hope that a question about happiness might just make her a little bit less sad.

In hindsight, I should have been better at interpreting her body language. Shortly after she settles down, she closes her eyes. After showing her ticket to the conductor, she closes them again. I approach her with mixed feelings. She doesn't really inspire conversation but there is also this altruistic feeling of wanting to help and cheer her up.

"Excuse me."

She opens her eyes and looks at me coldly. My self-confidence shrinks. I expect to see a glimmer of a smile appear on her face when I tell her about my happiness project but it is more like, "Are you nuts?" But I have started my course. I cannot give up.

"Would you please tell me three things that make you happy?"

"My children, reading, and sleeping." The eyes close shut.

I could, of course, tell you that I stopped here—it would have been the sensible thing to do. It is obvious that Lorena—that is her name—is in no mood for storytelling but I still have the slightest flicker of a hope that she will smile so I ask one more question.

"How old are your kids?"

"They are 17, 15, and 12."

She closes her eyes.

This time, I remain silent.

If my son quits using drugs
Tuesday, 2 February

It is bookstore time again! My eyes fall on a lady in her 50s who is sipping tea while scribbling in a journal.

"May I ask you a question, please?"

She looks up at me. She seems tired but kind.

"What makes you happy?"

"What would make me really happy would be for my 23-year-old son to stop being an addict. He has been using cocaine for seven years now."

She tells me how smart and handsome he is. He had finished high school and started university to become a lawyer. In the beginning he was a very functional addict able to handle school and drugs but then he lost interest in his studies.

"I don't know what to do anymore with him. We have spent so much money on sending him to rehab but nothing works. I keep asking myself what I did wrong as a parent. He grew up in a good home. Maybe the only thing that I did wrong was that I expected him to become somebody that *I* really wanted him to be. He is quite sensitive, and maybe this was too much pressure for him. Bad friends might also have had some influence."

"You should not blame yourself. Some of my friends suddenly discovered that their son had been a drug addict for 20 years, and they had always given him a loving and wonderful home."

"I know that I should not blame myself but it's hard not to do it. You see, he does not want to get clean. We are considering to stop paying for his apartment but what will happen to him? Our friends have no compassion and tell me that I should let him go but I cannot. I know I am co-dependent. I am his mother." She pauses for a while. "The second thing that would make me happy is that my family comes back together again."

"Are you divorced?"

"No, my husband and I have been married for many, many years. He works at the intensive care unit of a hospital where he sees so many deaths, so much youth dying from drugs. He gets very scared because he understands what it does to a person. My husband is very handsome, extremely honest, responsible but also very quiet and doesn't open up to me anymore. We no longer have much in common."

"You have only told me what things would make you happy in the future. Try to identify something that makes you happy in the present."

"Right now I just want to read and learn as much as I can so that maybe one day I can find a solution to my son's problems."

The next day I return to the bookstore. She is sitting at the same table.

"You know what made me happy yesterday?" she asks me. "Talking to you!"

A few years later she sends me an email announcing that her son is clean and doing well. This is true happiness!

Kushi! ("happy" in Bengali)
Wednesday, 3 February

The arrow of the Dunkin' Donuts sign is pointing to the right. A man bundled up with a large jacket, a sweater pulled up to this nose, a hat, and a pair of warm gloves is holding an eight-foot pole indicating the way to the store.

"Excuse me, sir, may I ask you a question?"

The sweater is pulled down. He stares at me without replying.

"I am Elisabeth. What's your name?"

"M.D.," he replies.

"Would you please name three things that make you happy?"

"Me happy," he says and looks at the pole.

"No. What makes you happy?

"Me, USA."

"Ah! Being in the USA makes you happy?"

"Me happy. Bangladesh, USA."

"How long have you been here?"

"Three months. New come. Green Card lottery."

"Are you happy here?"

"Yes, happy. Hard job. Job here no good. Work 43 hours a week. Seven days a week."

"I am happy when I read a book or eat," I say as I pretend to eat. "What makes you happy?"

"Eat rice. Happy."

I give up and laugh, "That's fine, M.D, as long as you are happy! I have to go now."

"See you again?" he asks.

"Yes, definitely," I smile.

On my way to the train that evening, I stop to see M.D. I have to give him something. I hand him a paper: Although my handwriting is a scrawl, he is able to recognize the word that I had written in Bengali. He looks at it, laughs, and says, *"kushi,"* which means "happy" in his language. I had gotten it from the internet.

"Kushi, kushi," I repeat several times.

"You talk good," M.D. replies.

For the love of money

Saturday, 6 February

The phone rings and ends my daydreaming.

"Elisabeth, have you had lunch yet?" It is Susan, my next-door neighbor. "I have made a big pot of beef stew. Why don't you join us?"

I happily accept the invitation. After lunch I sit down with Susan's daughter, Becky, a lanky 13-year-old girl with long blonde hair and coral blue eyes who loves to dance and do cheerleading.

"This is going to make me sound mean. I like money because it makes me feel in control, as if I can do anything. I mostly like the kind of money that I have to work hard for. I feel accomplished when I earn my own money. I don't want to have the stress of finances but just be free and independent, be able to pursue my own dream, go to Australia, travel the world, and become whatever I want."

She adds dreamily, "The second thing that makes me happy is summer. Summer makes me feel worry-free: I don't worry about work or anything else. I throw on clothes and go out of the house running wherever I want, with no limits. I love long summer nights when I can stay out watching the fireflies and eating ice cream. Finally, love makes me happy. I see love everywhere. Not family love and not boyfriend love either because you don't love anybody when you are 13."

Find what was lost
Tuesday, 9 February

"My dad used to say that in Judaism there is a saying that goes, 'when you lose something and you find it again, that makes you really happy.'"

Vlad, a NJ Transit commuter

My husband
Thursday, 11 February

Today the snow prevents me from going anywhere so I call my dear Aunt Grethe in Norway who is 80 years old.

"Tell me three things that make you happy."

"My adorable husband is my joy. Even though his short-term memory is getting worse, we have such a nice time together. I am grateful for this every day."

Whenever I think about soulmates, my Aunt Grethe and my Uncle Svein come to mind. They have been together for more than 60 years, and their love is stronger than ever.

"The second thing that makes me happy is to live in Norway, a safe and good country, and finally to be allowed to be healthy. At our age, in our circle, we see so much disease, so much death, that you really appreciate when you have a good health."

Peeping through windows
Tuesday, 16 February

"Looking at houses makes me happy. When I drive home at night, I often take another route so I can see different houses. I like to look through the windows, see how they furnish their homes, the paintings on their walls. I imagine the lives of the people who live there. The other night I saw one house with a red room, and further down the street we saw another house that also had a red room. When I used to walk the dog, I would feel like a little spy as I studied my neighbors' gardens and the interior of their homes. "

Shari, a colleague

Discoveries
Friday, 20 February

Today's "happiness date" is my Norwegian friend Thomas: tall, blue-eyed, blond, and well-spoken.

"Discoveries make me happy. We can discover so many things—books, people, paintings, places—but it is the unexpected pleasure of discovery that is the most attractive, discovery that happens haphazardly. Things or people you stumble over. My best memories are from discoveries," he tells me.

"What is your fondest discovery?"

"When I learned about my grandparents' secret love affair before they were married. I was always very close to my grandmother. One day when I was 12 years old she told me that she and her husband had a love affair during the two years prior to their marriage but that nobody knew about. She told me how they had met and how they used to write love letters to each other and send each other gifts. At that time they lived in different countries, her being Danish and him Norwegian. She pointed her finger to a cabinet in the corner and said, 'You see over there, in those drawers, are all our love letters and the gifts that we gave each other. When I no longer live, I want you to have them.'

"Years later, when my grandmother knew she was dying, she told me once again, 'Thomas, when I am gone, I want you to return to this house the day after I die, take these letters, without reading them, and burn each and every one of them. Let nobody read them. The gifts that we gave each other, I want to give to you.' She died on July 4, and on July 5 I went to her house, opened the cabinet, and placed each brittle, yellowed envelope, one by one, in the fire. I took their small, little gifts and lined them up on a shelf in my room. I don't recall all of them now but they were all engraved. I remember a pocket mirror and a powder case given to her by my grandfather. My grandmother had given him an engraved cigarette etui that said, 'In loving memory of the summer of 1946.'"

"Did you read any of the letters?"

"No, and nobody else did either. There are certain secrets that are not meant to be discovered."

A road sign
Tuesday, 23 February

"Happiness is the joy of seeing a road sign, indicating that you only have a few kilometers left until you reach home, when you have been biking the whole day and are tired."

Millan, Spanish cyclist

Remembering the good times

Friday, 26 February

It must be this season's biggest blizzard. Flurries keep falling over the skyscrapers in Manhattan. Roads are covered with slush and one foot of snow. The light is grey with small, white polka dots. The world is full of rubber boots in all shapes and colors, umbrellas shielding from the wind, snowflakes fighting for the airspace, people jumping over snowbanks and water puddles, plow trucks and workers throwing salt on the pavement. Once in a while cars drive by speedily and splash the pedestrians, who respond with angry insults.

Due to early dismissal at work, I have not been able to find a "happiness date." The train ride is my last chance. Enca, a lovely Brazilian widow, sits down next to me and shares her secret to a happy life.

"Happiness is a serene state of mind, built by remembering the good times. When you have good memories, they will serve as a pillar and sustain you in the present and contribute to your current happiness. Although my husband died 10 years ago, I was married for 40 wonderful years, and thinking about them now makes me very happy."

Train rides
Saturday, 27 February

"Books and train rides are sources of happiness. You must think this is an odd combination but I love to read on a train," says my friend Uju. "My best writing is also done there. It gives you a feeling of private space but at the same time a communal feeling. It's my favorite place to observe people. These days you can see everything over the internet—monuments, cities, rivers, things—but when you ride on a train, you can study people around you very naturally. The train shows me a window into people's lives. You discover their legends and their history. It is also a wonderful place to reflect.

"It's okay to ride the Amtrak but it feels a little bit sterile and claustrophobic. My best train rides are in India. Train rides in India are full of life. I fondly recall the sounds and the smells of vendors going through the aisles selling chai, magazines, and small snacks. I lean back as sugar cane fields, mustard fields, rice paddies, people, and rivers pass by. The scenery triggers spiritual moments for me."

"Is there one spiritual incidence that particularly struck you?"

"Yes, one day as I was travelling from Chennai to Mumbai, the train stopped in the middle of the night due to a mechanical problem. We were told that we would continue our trip in one hour so I went outside. The light of the moon was very strong that night. I walked into some fields, and at that point my eyes left my body. I was watching myself. What appeared to be a cobra suddenly crawled out from the fields, went around my ankles, and then left. To this day I am not sure whether the snake was real or a hallucination. This was a very strong experience."

Be the best gift you can be
Sunday, 28 February

"Happiness is having a true understanding of who you really are, knowing what you are willing to accept or not. Be true to yourself. Love yourself. Don't give up on yourself. As women, we need to be confident about ourselves. I used to be fat and did not like it. Weight does not help, and it is something you can control. Work on yourself. Be the best you can. Make yourself the best gift you can to the world."

Marie, Haitian girlfriend

March

Tapping into my spiritual voice
Monday, 1 March

A blonde lady, probably in her late 40s, is sipping a hot drink at one of the tables at the bookstore. She has kind, blue eyes and is eager to share her thoughts. Her name is Linda.

"Happiness to me is connecting with the inside," she says.

"How do you do that?"

"There are many ways of doing it. One is by writing. For instance, you could try the following for a certain amount of time. Take a pen and paper, then write, 'Dearest child of Love and Light, Elisabeth,' breathe, quiet your mind, and see what comes out on paper. After a while your thoughts, visions, and your highest consciousness will reveal themselves to you. You tune out the left side of the brain (logic) and tune in the right side (creativity). You clear out your ego, thoughts, the clutter, and tap into something spiritual inside you. You will find out that you are much more than what you believed you were—woman, mother, colleague, wife, and friend.

"Another way of tapping into my spiritual inner voice is by walking a labyrinth. Before entering the labyrinth, raise the question, then follow the path until you get to the middle. You center yourself, try to get an inner stillness. While you stand in its midst, you might have an answer, a vision or an idea, or none of the aforementioned. When you are ready, follow the path out again. In a labyrinth, you go in with the question, left brain, and out with what you have created, the right brain.

"You can also tap into your inner spiritual voice by listening to music or to a crystal or Tibetan bowl. Its sound is attuned to the vibrations in your body. Listening to this gong helps in balancing the vibrational elements of your body: heart-mind-soul. The more I listen to the Tibetan bell, the more pristine thoughts I get, the more I open my heart.

"Drawing and creating mandalas make me happy. Mandalas are sacred spaces and open communication with your inner self. When you color a mandala, breathe, follow your heart, and you will discover who you are. I draw a circle, and while I do so I quiet my mind. Sometimes I light a candle. This is my time to have a sacred union with myself. I focus on my breathing at the same time as I color the mandala. While you draw, you will access your subconscious self."

Fishing
Tuesday, 2 March

Not feeling too well, I decide to conduct a telephone interview with my dear cousin Axel in Norway.

"Let's start with the most important things first," he says.

We both laugh knowing very well what is coming next.

"My fishing trips. I must have been around seven or eight years old when I started fishing. I have a lot of fishing stories but there are particularly two that stand out.

"One time I was on the steppe of Hardanger and had been fishing the whole day without results. After night had fallen, I sat down near the river and threw out my line. The only sounds were the buzzing of the mosquitoes, who abound in that part of the country, and the gentle burble of the water. The moon was shining, and the sky was covered with stars. Suddenly one trout, then two, then three, hooked on to my fishing rod. It was magical!

"I do recall another time in the north of Norway. I had been walking yet another day without catching anything and the rain was coming down strong. But despite this, it was incredibly beautiful: grass-clad riverbanks, white birches, babbling rivers, and steep valleys. At night I stopped and threw my line out. I heard a loud splash and knew I had caught something big. Since I had planned on catching trout, the line of my rod was thinner than it would be for salmon so in order not to break it, I had to be very careful while reeling it in. It took me two hours and 45 minutes to haul it in. Although I was exhausted, it was all worth it: The fish weighed 7 kgs, and it happened so unexpectedly.

"If a fishing trip would only be about catching fish, I would have had more failures than successes. There are so many dimensions to a fishing trip. Even if I don't catch anything when nature is spectacular, it makes it all worthwhile. Just the fact of walking along the river puts you in a good mood. Being in nature and fishing, you do two kinds of travel: an outer travel, the scenery, as well as an inner travel. It gives you time to think and reflect upon life. Fishing gives you a positive aloneness, which is very different from the loneliness you can feel among people."

Remain healthy

Sunday, 7 March

I cross the lawn to my neighbor's house excitedly. I have been looking forward to my interview with Margaret for a long time. She is 98 years old and lives with her son and his wife. Despite having problems with her hearing and using a walker to get around, she is feisty, easy-going, and likes to laugh. All her life she worked as a nurse.

"The thing that really makes me happy is to remain healthy and to get this brace off."

During the past two years, she has had a couple of falls so now wears a brace around her waist.

"What is the second thing that makes you happy?"

She keeps thinking for a very long time.

"I really don't know what makes me happy. At my age what makes me happy?" She ponders some more.

"I guess that just to stay well and not fall makes me happy. My husband always used to say that I could fall over a pattern in the rug. Ha, ha!"

Find happiness in what you have
Tuesday, 9 March

I am swamped at work so when my Cuban colleague passes by, I grab him. He may be the only chance for a "happiness date" today.

"Manuel, what is happiness?"

"Happiness is being satisfied with what you have and appreciating what you have achieved in life. I remember when I was a kid in Cuba, two of my uncles were fishermen and lived very simple lives in a small fishing village. One day we invited them to La Habana and showed them around, wanting to share the best things that the capital had to offer. I was quite young at the time but I vividly remember that after only a short while, my uncles wanted to return to their little fishing village where there was no noise, only the sea, small houses, fishing boats, peace, and quiet. They knew that what they had made them happy."

"What was one of the happiest moments in your life?"

"When I got my first apartment in Cuba. You see, it is very difficult to get an apartment there. In my country the government does not build houses, only hospitals, post offices, schools, etc. The private sector does not build houses either. So if you want an apartment, you have to join a group or movement of micro-brigades: They will teach you how to build an apartment complex except for the roof, which will be put in by the government. For three years, I worked full time as a mason and plumber to be allowed to have this apartment. Later, I went abroad and was told that the apartment complex was finished and that I would have my unit. That day I was very happy!"

When Communism fell
Friday, 12 March

"I definitely think that the happiest moment in my life was when Communism collapsed in Ukraine in 1991. I had been the Executive Director of the first grassroots movement in Ukraine called "Greenland," which was a combined pro-independence and environmental movement, and the day we got our independence was truly amazing."

Iouri, Ukrainian friend

Love relationships

Thursday, 18 March

There is a feeling of spring in the air.

I am watching the skaters at the Rockefeller Center ice rink. A man with a white beard, black sunglasses, blue jeans, and a red polo is staring intently in the same direction. I study him discreetly from the corner of my eye, noticing a huge golden ring with a purple stone on his right hand.

"Excuse me, sir, would you mind if I asked you a few questions about happiness?"

"Not at all. I have been exploring this topic my whole life." His name is William, and he is a bishop.

"I think that what makes a person happy is to have love relationships. And I am not talking about sex. Every human being will endure a lot of hardship—sorrow, health problems, and interpersonal problems—but as long as you have love and quality relationships with the people you love and surround yourself with, you will be happy.

"The second thing that makes me happy is my love relationship with God. This really empowers me."

Our conversation steers into religion, and William shares some of his life story with me.

"I grew up in the streets in Philadelphia, and when I say the streets, I almost literally mean the streets. I was the last of eight children, and our family was very poor. My father was an alcoholic and was kicked out of the house. He would live in cars and just drink and smoke. Sometimes he would try to come back but my mother would throw him out. She was also an alcoholic and had several boyfriends. I didn't understand it at the time but in my later years, I understood that it must have been very difficult to raise eight children by herself.

"When I was 12 or 13 years old, I started believing in God. My family was Catholic but not practicing. When I was 17 years old, I was suicidal but then I started dating this sweet, young little girl. After just one or two months, I wanted to go on living and my passion to end my life simply vanished. I was really saved by the childish affection of a 15-year-old girl. Years later, I realized that this child's affection was enough water for a man dying of thirst because I did not have a father figure and my mother was dysfunctional due to alcoholism. I did not know that I was dying of lack of love.

"When I was 17, I started feeling a tremendous guilt for my body and my desires, and that life was hopeless. This sexual guilt was one of the reasons why, at the age of 19, I entered the Trappist order. I wanted to obtain innocence and purity and rid myself of this tremendous feeling of guilt. Of course, it was not the only reason. I also wanted to be united with God and go to Heaven when I die.

"At the Trappist monastery I basically lived without speaking to anybody for 11 years. The only times we were allowed to talk were for ten minutes to our confessor on Fridays, and once or twice a month to the abbot of the monastery. The rest of the time was spent chanting or in contemplation and meditation.

"After 11 years in the monastery, I got authorization to live in solitude, to become a solitary monk, in a cabin in the forest located three miles from the monastery.

"Once a month, from Friday to Sunday, I would go back to the monastery to shower, change my robes, and get a new stack of canned food.

"During the last part of my six years in this cabin, I got an awakening: I no longer suffered from sexual guilt. New preoccupations started to bother me, such as the nuclear arms race, the extermination of Native Americans, and the enslavement of African people. I felt guilty by association. I had had my direct special time with God; now I wanted to serve his people. I just wanted to be with those who were oppressed, not to save them, but to love them, and share their lives. I prayed about this for two years.

"After having lived six years in the cabin, the abbot of my monastery asked me if I would consider becoming the spiritual director, confessor, and chaplain for a sister Trappist Convent. I was not sure I would be able to be surrounded by so many women. You must remember, I had been living in celibacy and isolation for close to 17 years. But the abbot told me I could do it. So I did. I think these three years were among the most beautiful years of my life. I learned the beauty of women in a pure, innocent way.

"When my three years were up, they wanted me to renew my contract with them but I was afraid of liking it too much and of losing my prayer life so I returned to the hermitage for one year. However, my thoughts of living with the poor children of God would not leave me. In a monk's life there is always this tradition of pilgrimage, and for me, the most Holy Land is among the poor.

"I was finally allowed two years of leave of absence to do mission work in Bolivia and was sent for six months to Cochabamba where they have the best missionary school and language school in Bolivia. After speaking with a priest who had a mission in the midst of the indigenous people, I was allowed to live as a hermit there. This little village, called Aramasi, was two hours away from a main city.

"The natives, who were descendants of the Incas, spoke Quechua and lead lives in squalid poverty and in chronic sickness. There were no medical facilities there, only *curanderos* (witch doctors), so in addition to the role of *padre* (priest) and mentor, I also became the first aid man, doctor, and driver when I thought that a person needed to go to a hospital.

"Within walking distance there was a cinderblock church where I would offer Mass. The natives were Christians but had strong vestiges of their ancestral beliefs. I didn't think it was important. I just loved them, and I knew God loved them. Their poverty alone made them precious.

"I was installed there with the permission of the leadership of the village and would have services on Sundays. I spoke in Spanish, and my translators spoke in Quechua to the assembly. What I did not know then is that it would be impossible for them to understand what a contemplative monk was. I could have said, 'Well, I am not an ordinary priest but a contemplative monk.' But I couldn't really explain this due to the language barrier. To them, they just knew that I was a *padrecito*, which they had known for generations, as one of those white people who had stood between them and the landowners from whom they were serfs, and would speak for them and protect them as much as possible, while still being part of the lordship.

"After a few months, they were coming to my hermitage with all their problems. It took me a while to realize that this was what they always did with a *padre*. They asked me if I could appear with their leader at a court in Cochabamba to plead for the construction of a little waterway. I did it a few times.

"They also started bringing the sick and injured to my hermitage. There was no contact with the modern world so there were no band-aids or anything. If people were seriously ill, we tried to walk a few miles until we got to a dirt road and hoped that somebody would pass by so that they could bring them to a hospital.

"A couple of times a week, I would have people come to my door with compound fractures of the arm, and I learned a new Spanish phrase, 'I fell from my field,' because the small patches that they cultivated were on such a slope that if you lost your balance, you tumbled down hundreds of feet.

"They had awful skin diseases because they had no soap, no running water. They washed and drank from the same water sources where the animals relieved themselves. Many were living with chronic Chagas disease, intestinal parasites that many were dying from in their 40s and 50s. There was disease all over the place, and the visible ones, the skin diseases, were contagious and spread by touching. They had it on their feet, their hands, and their faces. They would bring me people with scabby places on their bodies, which were very easy to treat. My life changed. I was supposed to be a contemplative monk but I became a field medic.

"One time four men knocked on my door. They were carrying a home-made stretcher made out of strong branches with a blanket thrown around. On it lay a woman who was burning up with fever, with a full-term baby that she could not deliver." He sighs. "That was more than I could deal with so I put her in the back of my Jeep and drove her to the nearest little hospital and got her admitted. They induced labor, and her life was saved but the baby was lost.

"While that was happening, my first disciple, BJ, came down from New York City. He said, 'Father William, my ministry is expanding. Let me challenge the men that I minister to in New York to build a little hospital here.'

"It took about a year and a half to two years. It was very difficult to get the materials and to develop a budget plan with a resident doctor and a nurse but it happened. And it's still there!

"Now I was in charge of something, and had to go to the United States every year to explain what we were doing so they would continue to support our doctor and nurses. All seemed to be well and good until I went into the city of Cochabamba. I usually stayed at a convent there, where they had a spare room. I would pick up materials, food, and toilet paper. I stayed there at most for three days, then loaded up my Jeep and drove back out.

"While in Cochabamba, I went over to the American Missionary Convent to meet with Sister Columba, a dear, dear friend, and we drove to a park in Cochabamba. While we were conversing, two men from each direction came to the side of our Jeep, and I thought to myself 'Oh! It's closing time for this public park!' But they were robbers. They pulled me out of the car and started beating on me, kicking me in the stomach. We didn't know whether we were going to live or die.

"They left me on the ground there. We thought they would steal our car but they didn't. I made a vow that night that if I was staying in Bolivia, I was not going to meet people on the street but at a missionary center house.

"That took us into phase two of my mission in Bolivia. In 24 months, we had a missionary house in the city of Cochabamba, with electricity and flush toilets. It was called 'La Morada' (the Dwelling Place). It became a retreat house for locals and a reception house for people from the United States. I would come to the city once or twice a month for two to three days.

"I was about to go back to Aramasi from Cochabamba when the local neighborhood organization came and said, 'Oh *Padre*, we are going to start a medical *posta'*—which is a clinic where they just have a nurse and maybe a doctor—'in the city of Cochabamba. We know the government will take our supplies and cheat us. Will you just oversee it, just keep it honest?'

"I did not want to but I could not refuse. I only had to come up with $500 more a month. I had a nun who was going to do it. It would be a wonderful ministry for her. The nun and I went over with the leadership of the neighborhood and saw this building, which had just been put up and had five rooms. We decided we were going to do this.

"But there was a back door. I opened it, and there was a brick pavement that went about 50 yards to another large one-story building, a state-operated orphanage.

"Here is where my life takes a major change. We walked across these 50 yards of brick pavement, and the closer I got to the building, the greater the stench became.

"The first greeting I got was from an emaciated-looking dog with matted hair. There was writing all over the walls. Finally, a Spanish woman came out; she was the director of this orphanage. I introduced myself. She had one helper, a Quechua girl. She was the only staff. Surely, she didn't not know anything about cleanliness. The director started crying to me, 'The babies are dying. We cannot do anything. There are no funds.' I followed her around. We went into the infants' room: Maybe 20 or 30 cribs stood side by side. In some of the cribs, there were two babies; one of them contained three babies.

"I was appalled at what I was seeing, and I looked at one baby.

His eyes were staring blankly toward the ceiling, mouth open with flies walking around the lips. It was an atrocity!

"I called my friend BJ in New York, and told him what I had seen. I didn't really want to do this but my friend said, 'We cannot just walk away from this.'

"Our first approach was to bring food and medicines to the orphanage until we found out that the things we were bringing in, state administrators were carrying out to sell someplace else.

"One day BJ came down with 150 stuffed animals. He called it 'Operation Teddy Bear.' The director got the children—there were children up to ten years old in this orphanage—in a small line to receive their stuffed animal one by one. It was a sight to behold! Well, you went in there a month later, and there were no more stuffed animals. Even the stuffed animals they confiscated!

"At the same time I hired this Bolivian couple who were both pediatricians. They were doing the best they could but one day they told me, 'Father William, we cannot treat these children. We need a segregation unit so that sick children who come in can be segregated and treated before being placed in the general population.'

"All babies that came in were sick. We had babies that were picked out of trashcans, abandoned by the roadside, hung on the fence of the orphanage by a blanket. So we raised money and got the isolation unit so these doctors can control the infections, right? But within six months, the doctors were saying, 'Father William, the government keeps sending more babies. Now they are putting more children in the isolation unit because they have nowhere else to put them so we are back to square one.'

"I got a lawyer to write a letter—this takes weeks, months— saying that these children were wards of the state and not our children, and we basically just wanted to serve them. But in our original contract, we would determine the number of children we could care for in the facility. We told them that they had not fulfilled their obligation, and they were creating overpopulation, which jeopardized the health of all of the children. Therefore, they should either limit the population to 110 or we would withdraw our services.

"I never questioned this until we got a letter saying, 'you can leave.' They had their own plan. They were using that orphanage as a place of destitution, to get visitors who saw it to make donations and in-kind contributions, which the staff in the administration would confiscate. While we were there, the children were being treated well but the officials lost that source of revenue.

"We decided that the only way we could save these babies was to have an orphanage of our own. Then began another two years of labor, and we had our own orphanage, of which we celebrated the 25th anniversary two years ago. We didn't duplicate the model of a large orphanage with 50 or 100 children. We chose the family model with independent dwellings for between four to ten children and a permanent resident *mama*. It was called Children's Village.

"I lost two of my dearest and closest emotional friends, Mother Columba, who was called to be an abyss in England, and Mary Mahoney, who was killed in a flashflood, together with two others. They were my emotional support. Then, the brother missionaries that I had from Iowa gave their mission church in Cochabamba over to the Bolivian clergy and returned to Iowa. My fellowship community was disappearing. I was left alone, with nothing but this expanding economy, clinic, orphanage, and retreat house. We had 100 people working for us. It was way beyond what I could do.

"I started getting sick. At the worst point I had two chronic, resistant internal infections. I was losing weight, I was sick, I was not sleeping, I was unhappy."

He pauses.

"How many years had you been there by that time?"

"Six or so. We were going to hire another nurse for the new orphanage that we got going. I interviewed this woman in our parlor, and you need to know I was not thinking marriage, relationship, or sex. I didn't do porn but I was incredibly lonely. I was so lonely when I came back from one of those yearly trips from New York so I went to our little chapel in Cochabamba. Sister Columba had made the curtains for the windows in the chapel. Do you know I went over and was practically hugging the curtains because I missed her so much? I was in bad shape. I would never let her know that. I was haunted by Sister Columba. As I was interviewing this Bolivian nurse, she looked at me and said, '*Padrecito*, what's the matter?' And I replied, 'I am just so lonely.' She got up, came over to me, sat on my lap, hugged me, and caressed my face. In my right mind I would have said 'wait a minute' but I didn't. It was some affection. I was about 49 years old. I was not sexually active so I didn't have any experience with that. But it does not take much for a man to cross a threshold where he commits a sexual sin. I went to my confessor and told him what had happened. He said to me, 'Look, Willy, you are burnt out. You need to get yourself back together. You need to get out of Bolivia. You are sick, physically and emotionally.'

"I called up BJ in New York. 'I am burnt out. I am losing my moral self-control. I must have a break.' He asked if I could stay until August so that he could keep his promise to two graduates from a university that he had been mentoring and whom he had told could come and study with me in June and July.

"I took it to thought and prayer and came up with a plan. If I imposed a curfew on myself so that I would not leave La Morada building for anything short of absolute necessity, and if I took care of my health, sleep, medication, and prayer, it might be possible. When they came, it changed everything. I could focus on them. I was a spiritual father again. I was ok. I never returned to that nurse's house."

"Father William, I am bringing it back to your love relationship with Jesus. Just like Jesus felt abandoned by God when he was crucified, did you feel God's presence, or did you feel that He had abandoned you?"

"I felt like I had abandoned Him, and when you feel that way, you can't let in feelings of being loved by God so I was not getting much comfort from that direction. I never despaired of His mercy. I believed God was with me but it was not emotionally close.

"Here is where Susan comes in. I go back to the United States. I was on the night flight out of South America with Miami as the first stop. I stared into the darkness through the small windows and planned what I should do. I could close the clinic in Aramasi but if I did, babies would die. I could give the retreat house in Cochabamba, La Morada, to the diocese, and they would be happy to receive it, and then I could return to the monastery where I was happy, successful, respected, and not tempted. But we had 100 families who were getting their livelihood from the mission now. It was not black or white.

"Upon my arrival to the U.S., I did a tour of ten or 12 cities, returned to New York, and got ready to go back to Bolivia. BJ told me there was a doctor in the city who wanted to do a medical mission and would like to interview me about how she would fit into the program. But she was leaving the next day so I had to meet her for breakfast in the morning.

"The next morning we meet at a diner. I wait at a booth, and a smart-looking, dark-haired woman in a trench coat—it was snowing heavily outside—her feet clicking on the tile floor, comes over to my table and starts talking to me. This is a sweet thing, and I say this as a spiritual testimony. I had no concept of what was going to happen because my method of interviewing is always the same: 'What's your background, and what's your interest? Why do you want to do work in our mission?'

"She is an Episcopalian who got into a bad marriage for the wrong reason when she was 20 to get away from her mother. After seven years of abuse and infidelity, she got divorced and dedicated herself to medicine, and now she is in her second to last year of residency as a general surgeon. She had given up on relationships. Her idea was: 'My patients will be my family.' She had a great heart. She had done short-term medical missions in Central America, and she was thinking to begin with part-time mission work in Bolivia for the summer. She was 39 years old. I was 50.

"As I am listening to her story—I can see she is a believer, she loves the Lord—I start having a secret conversation with God. Here is the tenor of the conversation that she doesn't hear: 'Lord, maybe if I loved a woman like this in marriage, it would give me the strength that I need to continue to serve You and Your poor in the world.'

"I felt attraction. This is the first time in my life at 50 years I ever did this: I said, 'Lord, I am going to listen to my feelings of attraction, and I will go with them as far as You want me to go.' That means I am going to marry this woman or zero. I don't say this to her. But at that booth at the Gemini Diner on 2nd Avenue and 34th Street, for the first time in my life, I felt attracted to a good woman, and I let myself go with it as far as God wanted me to go. After two and a half hours, I walk her to her little car. I ask her, 'Can I give you a hug before you go?' 'Sure,' she replies. So there we are, standing in front of her car in overcoats between the snowbanks; I hug her. Normally, you hug and then you let go but I didn't. I said, 'I am having a hard time letting you go!' This threw her into a total confusion, silently wondering, 'What does that mean? Is he coming onto me?' It was confusion time for Susan! She got in the car and drove away.

"I went back to BJ and admitted, 'I really felt love for that woman.'

"On December 25 I was in Philadelphia at my sister's, and Susan was back in New York. I got the chance to go to New York to spend several hours with her. She was trying to figure out what was going on. It would be a death sentence to get involved with a senior monk, missionary, and priest! But anyway, I guess she was going with her feelings, too. I am with her, we eat, get some wine, share our life stories, we don't yet talk about our love for each other.

"I go back to Bolivia, and we start a long-distance relationship. She sends these little mini-cassettes, and once a week we would have a Saturday conversation that she would pay for. She didn't tell me then, only later, that she had to get a payment plan because we talked for half an hour. I only had $50 a month for spending money.

"After a few months, on a phone conversation, Susan asks me, 'William, how would you describe our relationship? Is this a priest-parishioner, a penitent-spiritual director, or is it man and woman?' I reply, 'Sure, it is man and woman relationship.' Then there was a silence. I consciously and intentionally courted her but my problem was, 'Is it possible for a Roman Catholic priest? Is it immoral, wrong, sinful even, to think about such a thing?' I told her that. I am too old to mess up my life and hers. We entered a prayer contract. She did not make any demands on me. Susan is very much a take-charge person but in this instance, she left all the moves to me.

"In Bolivia, I prayed to God, 'Lord God, don't let me mess up my life at 50. You have been so good to me. Take my life, don't let me live to destroy it.' I fasted. I talked to my religious colleagues but they could not receive it. There were some wonderful nuns living at La Morada but they were all against it, and they turned against me.

"I wrote a letter to my second spiritual director when I was a monk. He was a wonderful man of God whom I admired, looked up to, loved, and I knew he loved me. He had been sent to a Trappist monastery in Peru. I asked him if I could have a retreat with him for a week.

"I said, 'I will be completely transparent with you. My question is only this: Is it against the will of God that I should consider a possible call to marry this woman?'

"After a great fellowship for a whole week, he said, 'Willy, there is no theological, biblical, nor spiritual reason why you should not be permitted to marry this woman, if that's God call to you. But if you do this, you are going to be nothing. What are you going to do? You have no profession. You are 50 years old.' He was right about that. He didn't want me to end up with nothing to do, or no place in the world. I took that in.

"Thomas Merton, one of the most important Roman Catholics of the 20th century, had a love relationship with a nurse. He fell in love when he was about my age, and he wrote her beautiful love poetry.

But he was under pressure from the Pope and everybody else not to develop this relationship. They warned him that the whole world would be scandalized if he left the monastery for a woman. At the end, he writes her a letter saying, 'There is no place in the world for us.' There was no place in the traditions of men for them. His life was cut short by an accidental death on a trip to the Far East but he had not terminated that relationship. What might have happened if he had lived to see it through?

"I went back to Bolivia. I prayed and fasted. I asked people to pray for me. One of the nuns hurt me so badly. I had been such a good friend and priest to her, and she said to me, 'No one can be in the Holy Spirit and behave the way you are behaving.' The nun who had worked in our orphanage told me not to visit. I was rejected all around.

"My plan was, at the end of that year, to go to the monastery, tell the abbot, and ask him if I could spend six months to a year there while cutting off all communication with Susan. I would be a hermit if they let me or lead a regular life as a monk in the community. At the end of that time, I would see if she would still be there, and what my decision would be. I thought it was a leading from God to do that. But I am sorry to tell you that the abbot, who was a friend, refused, 'Father Willy, the community cannot handle that. I am asking you not to tell people because it is too scandalous, even your thinking about marriage.'

"I lined up 12 hours of Christian relationship counseling in New Jersey for Susan and me, seeking an answer to the question: 'As a Christian counselor, do you see any reason, either spiritual, religious, biblical, or psychological, why I should not be able to marry Susan?'

"Some friends had told me I was having a late mid-life crisis. After finishing our sessions with this counselor, the conclusion was: 'you are an unlikely couple, you are very, very different, but you both have individual strengths that, if you play to them psychologically speaking, you have as much chance of having a happy marriage as anybody else.'

"During this period, I reread the Bible from Genesis to Revelation, with one question, 'What is God saying about marriage?' It begins in a marriage with Adam and Eve and ends in marriage with Christ and the Bride Church in Revelation.

"A year after our first meeting I was sitting in the office in New York with BJ and his wife, who love me very much, but they are strongly against me leaving my celibate life, and they don't know how I am going to emerge from this dilemma.

"BJ's wife, Sheila, said to me, 'Father William, it is getting near Christmas. You should think about getting a Christmas present for your friend Susan.' You must realize that I had not bought anybody a Christmas gift for the past 30 years—monks don't do that. So I smiled 'That must be fun! Maybe I can get her a dress or something like that.' But Sheila told me, 'Oh no, no, no! That's inappropriate.' Here is the moment of revelation. I thought for a few seconds. Then I came out with this idea: 'I know what I am going to get her: an engagement ring.' I had never thought about that before this moment. Shocked, they both looked at me. Sheila replied, 'Do you know what you are saying?' I said, 'Yes, I will give it to her and, if she takes it, we will get married.' At that moment, I totally knew that I wanted to marry Susan, and that it was right in God's eyes. That certainty never changed.

"Did you need to get your contract as a priest annulled?"

"Well, I realized that in the church I was going to lose my friends, my position, and my priestly duties. I was going to accept all this, and that I was going to get laicized if I renounced the priesthood, and I thought that, as a good Catholic, it would be the right thing to do. I would still be a lay Catholic, right? But I did not want to give up the priesthood. I really loved the Eucharist. My first attitude was to just submit to the church's regulation. If a priest wants to get married, he has to give up his priesthood. But one evening I was meeting with a man who I first ministered to, and who became a minister to me. He later died of AIDS. He had been a Methodist minister for many, many years, raised a family, but came out of the closet as a gay man. He was totally humiliated in that culture. When he was near death, by a failed suicide attempt, God came to him. He became a celibate gay person and was reinstated in the ministry before he died. I was staying with him at the time. I told him about my engagement ring revelation. He said, 'Father William, are you going to join another denomination? If you did, you would be able to continue to serve in the body of Christ.'

"I thought about that. The Roman Catholic Church is the body of Christ but so is the church of all believers everywhere. So I pursued, and was eventually accepted in the Episcopalian priesthood. Once I made the decision, I had to start informing my loved ones, my family, the nuns at the convent, and my brother monks whom I had lived with for 25 years. Some were angry, others heartbroken; very, very few affirmed my decision. I knew I was breaking hearts. It was so physically painful to me. I had a list of people I was going to explain it all to. I wrote three or four letters but I just could not do any more. That pain was physical, in the chest. I lived with this pain until I got married, and then it went away. But it was a terrible pain of separation and loss. However, let nothing interfere with love, right?

"That's my testimony. I want to emphasize the fact of how a woman's love makes a man alive. A girl saved my life when I was 17, and when I was 50, Susan's affection opened me up to life that was never opened to me before. And in between, I had these affectionate celibate relationships with half a dozen different nuns, and they were very important to me. They were chaste and pure. But the affection was life-giving.

"But I also know that I have never, ever, abandoned my passion for the pursuit of God. It is with me now, as much as when I was a monk. It is just that the expression of it is different. As a monk, I sought the love of God instead of all things. As a husband and father, I seek God's love in and above all things."

Surviving cancer
Friday, 19 March

The Rockefeller Center is even more crowded today than yesterday. I have circled three quarters of the square when I notice a lady in a wheelchair wearing red pants and a flowery shirt, enjoying the skaters while sipping a soft drink. Her name is Geraldine, and she is visiting from Ireland with her husband. As she removes her sunglasses, I see kind, blue eyes.

"Geraldine, tell me three things that make you happy."

"Being alive, living, and surviving cancer. I was diagnosed with breast cancer in 2006, then it went to the bones. I am just praying that it does not go to the organs. Every three months I have CT scans done. So far, so good. I have had a lot of operations since then. I had an artificial hip put in recently and have a hard time walking. That's why I am now sitting in a wheelchair."

As I ask, "What is happiness?" she becomes pensive and gets a dreamy expression on her face.

"Happiness is being aware of the beauty around you, being able to see and appreciate living in the now. It is enjoying what I have got."

"I admire your strength, Geraldine," I tell her. "You seem to have a very positive outlook on life." But considering all she has told me I hesitate before I ask, "Are you happy?"

"I am happier now than before my diagnosis," she says, and I am stunned.

She suddenly turns around. "Elisabeth, this is my husband, Tony. Tony, this is Elisabeth. She is just asking me some questions about happiness."

A middle-aged man with thick, grey hair, an eagle nose, and a warm smile greets me. He has just been on the top of the Rockefeller Observation Deck.

"Would you mind if I interviewed you, once I am done talking with Geraldine?" I ask him.

"No, that would be fine. I will let you two finish while I go look at the ice-skaters."

Geraldine continues. "Where was I? Yes, I am happier now than before I got sick. This was a wake-up call, and the knowledge that I would die sooner than anticipated made me focus more on the now.

Things I used to worry about in the past do not affect me anymore. I pay less attention to small grievances. To the point that sometimes I almost become intolerant toward people, when they keep complaining about things that, in my eyes, are insignificant." She laughs apologetically.

"Where do you find your strength?"

"I rediscovered my faith. This helps me tremendously. Another source of strength is from within me. I never thought I would be able to go through these kinds of ordeals—all these operations, the chemotherapy, the radiation, take all these pills—but I am! I have found strength in myself through my dealing with my sickness. My husband's support is unwavering. He cooks for me every day and does everything that needs to be taken care of in the house. What makes me happy also is the amount of support that I receive from friends and family. I have so many people who pray for me."

We both get teary-eyed. She raises her arms toward me to give me a hug, and we stay like this for a while.

"How do you think your husband is coping with this?"

"He doesn't say much about it. He does whatever he can for me. Sometimes he will get angry for no reason. For instance, he yelled the other day that it was hard to find one's way around in New York. But I think that is probably some bottled up frustration. No marriage is perfect but we are having a nice life together."

Tony returns and just as discreetly as he had left when I was talking to his wife, Geraldine starts her electric wheelchair and takes off.

"What three things make you happy?" I turn to Tony and ask.

"The first thing that makes me happy is my relationships. Not only my wife and family, but all my relationships, even the bad ones, because I can learn from them. When a relationship is difficult, I always take something away from it.

"The second thing that makes me happy is me."

"What do you mean by that?"

"Well, nobody but me can make me happy. I am able to be happy by being okay with me, by accepting myself as I am, even the bad things that I like less about myself.

"The rest of what makes me happy centers around what I mentioned before. But if you want me to say a third thing, I guess it would be good quality material items, such as a nice home, a nice car, travel in comfort, etc."

Usually, I would never tell the husband what his wife had said or vice versa but today I feel compelled to hear his version of the story.

"Tony, your wife told me that she is happier since she was diagnosed with cancer than before. Are you happier now, too?"

"No, I would not say that. I just take one day at a time. I am generally happy. If I didn't have a sad day, I wouldn't know when I had a good one. I try to do the right thing in life and for my wife. Medically, there's nothing I can do. Good doctors are taking care of her. But as long as I do what I feel I am supposed to do, and Geraldine is happy, then I am happy."

You are your own creator of happiness

Saturday, 20 March

"You have to create happiness yourself. You don't wake up, and pouf! Happiness is suddenly there! You have to make your own happiness. Don't expect anybody or anything to make you happy. In order to create your own happiness, you have to find what you value in life. I value human beings, helping and caring for others, good deeds, good relationships, and if I can be part of changing their lives to the better, this will make me happy. If I see a child that is hungry and I can feed him or her, that makes me happy. In short, happiness is making sure that your life is filled with values that are important to you.

"With old age and hopefully, more wisdom, happiness is doing things that enhance my quality of life. I want to enjoy every moment of my life."

Mary Alice, Haitian girlfriend

Do not lose hope
Sunday, 21 March

"Happiness is feeling content with no outstanding unfulfilled needs, being loved and loving somebody else, the absence of worry. However, I do not expect to be happy all the time. Life is comprised of good and bad, and I know that the bad times will eventually pass. I might be unhappy today but I can still envision being happy in the future. Today might suck but it won't last forever. You can be unhappy but not lose hope."

Fran, a neighbor

Studying

Tuesday, 23 March

The weather is gloomy and grey; it seems to mirror the way I feel. I find myself reflecting on some of the lessons learned from my "happiness dates," and this gives me strength.

The bookstore is crowded. A young Asian man is sitting alone at a table drinking coffee and reading a book. I gently approach him.

He gets up, reaches out his hand, and says promptly, "Hi, I am David. Sit down. I would gladly answer some questions.

"Helping others make me happy. I love volunteering," he tells me. "The second half of last year I started tutoring college kids in math." He hesitates briefly before continuing, "Studying. You see, I dropped out of school for two years. Let me explain. My mother lives in California and my father in China. From fourth grade to eighth grade, I lived with my father but I was the worst student in the class. I didn't care. He decided to send me to my mother for ninth grade. That October I got a phone call from my grandmother that would change my life. She told me, 'David, it is not easy for your mom to raise you alone. She has done a lot of sacrifices for you. Be a good boy and study hard. Make her proud.'

"Two days later she ended her life. Due to kidney failure she needed to go for dialysis several times a week, and she was tired. This phone call marked a turn-around in my life. I decided that I would study really hard and be the best I could. When I finished high school, I was the kid with the best grades in my class. I went to a good college, was overly ambitious and, being a perfectionist, always thought I could do better.

"I had good grades but was not happy. I started skipping classes and locked myself in my room. After one week my roommate took me to the psychologist who said I was depressed. I quit school for two years, went back to live with my father in China, and did a lot of stupid things. I drank, smoked, snuck out of the house at night, lied to my friends, gambled, and lost all the money. In China, gambling is illegal except for in Macaw so I joined the underground casinos. It was dangerous; they were owned by the mob. I lost hope and thought I would never be able to go back to school. I remember seeing all the American interns in their nice suits and envying them. I hated myself. Finally, in September 2009, my dad sent me back to my mom. I enrolled at the college I had been to before and, to my surprise, I found that I still understood math and was capable of studying. It was wonderful."

Thinking of paradise

Thursday, 25 March

"Are you ready, Mariam?" I smile at my Ethiopian colleague.

She moves her chair closer to mine and lowers her voice. "I love seeing the sea, the sun, and the greenery outside. When I lived back home, many of my friends lived in different parts of the country, and we would travel together sometimes to resorts near the biggest lake in Ethiopia called Lake Tana or visit the numerous churches that my country is so well-known for. I remember driving through green fields on desolate roads, bordered with eucalyptus, pine, and palm trees. At times we could see the mountains in the distance. We would bathe in natural hot water springs. I also enjoy reading the Bible and meditating."

She stops, and a flicker of a shy smile crosses her face. "I don't meditate in a traditional sense of the word. I just think about Paradise. When I try to imagine Paradise, I feel happy and my worries disappear. According to the Bible, it is a place with no suffering or trouble and where everything is made of gold and silver."

"When did you start thinking about Paradise?"

"I think I have always been aware of Paradise because in my country people are very religious and we always go to church. But I believe I seriously started thinking about it when I came alone to this country whilst my husband remained in Ethiopia. It was very hard for me. Thinking of Paradise made me feel better. I remember beginning to wonder how Paradise would be, and the more I thought about it, the less scared I became of death. Before, when loved ones died, I had always been very sad but when I realized that they actually went to Heaven, I felt better. This hope helped me a lot when my father died."

Doing philanthropic work
Friday, 26 March

"Dedicating my life to helping others and doing philanthropic work make me happy. It doesn't matter if I don't bring home a huge paycheck at the end of the month, as long as I feel that I contribute in making a difference, in making the world a better place to be. Whenever I feel that I have done something good, I feel better. I do political fund-raising for the ASPCA, Amnesty International, Save the Children, the NRDC (an environmental group), and soon I will also raise money for the Democratic party. I have a 90-hour work week."

Alex, ASPCA fund-raiser

When you see a new day
Tuesday, 30 March

I feel lost in the water. Heavy raindrops are falling on the grey mirror-like tiles in Bryant Park. Tall plane trees sway from side to side. The slight tapping of the rain on my umbrella join the chorus from a large copper fountain. I am alone in the park. Wait! Between two lines of trees, budding daffodils and bottle-green tables and chairs, a man entirely dressed in a yellow rain overall is picking up papers and plastic bottles with his broom and dustpan.

I try to catch his attention but his head is downcast as he focuses on scooping up a resistant paper, refusing to be extracted from the leaves of a tiny bush.

"Excuse me, may I ask you a question?" I finally say.

He looks up. His name is Bernard, and he is from Jamaica. I notice an accent as he speaks. He must be in his late 50s.

"What three things make you happy?"

"To be alive, to have a job. You cannot be happy without money, and you don't want to depend on anybody, and then a relationship makes you happy. I met a lady the other day."

He seems guarded so I do not probe further.

"Bernard, what is happiness?"

"We are here. We can see another day, the sun, or the rain. Each day is blessed."

April

My dogs
Friday, 2 April

"Oh hello, Elisabeth!" Beth, one of my neighbors, opens the door. She is 70 years old, feisty, and speaks with a southern drawl. "Come on in! Let's sit in the living room."

Morgan, their ten-year-old Portuguese Water Dog, follows us.

"My dogs make me happy," she says passionately. "I was raised with dogs down in West Virginia. We had an Irish Setter, two English Setters, and one Pointer. My father was a very manly man and loved to play golf and hunt. This is where I got my love of dogs."

"When did you get your first dog?"

"We got our first dog, Magnolia, a Bassett Hound, nine months after we got married. When the Berlin Wall was set up, my husband Charlie, who was an officer at that time, was sent to Bavaria. We had to leave the dog with my mother. Upon our return we got our second dog, Jemima. She was a Puli, with black dreadlocks, very smart, and sweet. Toward the end of her life, she was blind and deaf. We would let her out in the back of the garden but she would only walk a little bit away from the house because she would get lost. When you approached her to pet her, she would get startled since she couldn't hear you. When she was 12 years old, we had to put her down.

"It took us a while to mourn Jemima but we realized we couldn't live without a dog so we bought another Puli that we named Sadie. One day I took her to the groomer and saw a gorgeous dog on the grooming table. They told me it was a Portuguese Water Dog. I went home and told my husband, 'Charlie, I have just seen the most incredible dog in the world!'

"Portuguese water dogs are not too easy to come by so I started doing research and, after a while, found a breeder who sold them. Charlie and I went to see them. They were beautiful. There was particularly one that caught my eye. The lady who was selling them said to me, 'I will only sell you this one if you will show her in dog shows.' Charlie immediately answered, 'Let's take another dog.' But I was adamant the little black furry one was the one I wanted. So we bought her with a stipulation in the sales contract that she would be a show dog. Pretty soon, Abby had won everybody over. When she was one and a half, she became a champion and was shown in Virginia, the Carolinas, and New England. She had three litters and 29 puppies."

Maximize your gifts
Saturday, 3 April

The café at Barnes & Noble is busy. After circling twice, my eyes dwell on a lady who is reading magazines. Her name is Nancy.

"What is happiness to you?" I ask her.

"I guess it's a contentment with the gifts you have been given. For instance, I am good at cheerleading and in motivating people to achieve certain things. One of your gifts might be that you are good in interviewing people and writing about it. I don't believe when people tell me, 'Oh, but I don't have any gifts.' We all have gifts: We just have to discover them.

"I believe happiness is to be aware of your gifts, which have been given to us by some power greater than us, and it's up to you to do the best you can with them. This will lead to contentment.

"Happiness is a mixture of Hinduism and Christianity, the Hinduism part being of not striving, of accepting where we are and that it is good, while the Christianity part is being thankful for being, for what we have. However, we should not forget other people's plights and sufferings. We have an obligation to lessen each other's suffering, whether it be earthquakes or broken relationships. When attention is taken off myself, I am able to work within the good areas of myself and to use my gifts for a greater good, and this makes me happy."

"Are you happy, Nancy?"

"Searching for happiness can contribute to your unhappiness. It depends on where and how we search for it. I always tell my students, 'You are the most important things in the universe but, at the same time, you are insignificant to the universe.' If you can come to terms with this, you can get contentment.

"When kids are about 16 to 17 years old, they start realizing that there is something else out there, and this will prompt excitement, apprehension, and sometimes fear. I think we do kids and students a disservice by all the affirmations we always give them. They have to figure out how to operate between the boundaries of being the most important things in this universe but, at the same time, of being insignificant. If you get stuck on either of them, you will not have a full and complete life and you will be very disappointed. We have to realize when to be assertive, and when to go with the world."

"Name a few things that make you happy."

"Teaching and making music as well as research. I teach Music and Western Culture to high school students. I also play the organ and piano and teach music to choral singers. I am currently doing my second PhD. My first one was on sacred music, which was mostly church music, but I also incorporated American spirituals."

"American spirituals? I have always heard about 'Negro Spirituals?' Are there other 'Spirituals?'"

"That's a very good question. These days there are a lot of explorations of people's genetic background and, in the same way, many studies are being made on the DNA of spirituals. In Northern England and Ireland, one can find psalm singers in Gaelic who have the same style as the spirituals performed by the rural white, black, and Indians in Alabama. My second PhD is essentially about that: American Spirituals."

"What are some of the happiest moments in your life?"

"When I succeed in performing a piece very well, it is within those moments that I feel an intense happiness. It's like for a while the curtain splits, I get to see a glimpse of truth, like a divine moment, and then it slams shut. This happens particularly with *La piece d'orgue* of Bach."

She stops and thinks.

"When I have accomplished another degree is also an extremely happy moment."

"You mentioned that your first doctorate was about sacred music and spirituals?"

"Yes, I was looking at how spirituals have been used in Christian worship. I also looked at sacred places."

"What is the relationship between 'sacred places' and 'music'?"

"Music is the manifestation of something spiritual. Sacred music is the music of the spheres. The Greek believed that everything that has '*anima*'—that is, living—whether we can see the movement or not has a sound. I went to the Stonehenge in England and to the labyrinth in Chartres to listen to their music."

"Nancy, can you hear music everywhere you go?"

"Yes, I can hear it everywhere but sometimes I tune it out. It's the music of the spheres."

She suddenly closes her eyes and seems to focus. After 30 seconds, she opens them again.

"Did you hear any music now, here at Barnes & Noble?"

"Yes, it is kind of a wind blowing. I have been to the Sistine Chapel a lot of times, maybe 12 times, because I have taken students on trips there. It took me a while to hear the music there but I eventually felt it."

I wish this conversation will never end. We proceed to talk about folksongs.

"Most folksongs are written in the key of F major, which is the most human key: It represents the human condition," Nancy says. *La Piece d'orgue* is written in G major, which is the key of beauty. The little folksongs are almost always in F because they are so easy to sing."

The next moment, in close to perfect Norwegian, she sings a very old, traditional Norwegian folksong called *Per Spelmann Han Hadde ei Einaste Ku* (Peter Spellman He Had a Single Cow).

There was no end to my amazement that day!

The day I scored my first soccer goal
Sunday, 4 April

"Caroline, Caroline!" I holler as I see the 13-year-old daughter of our neighbors pass by on her bike.

She stops and sits down next to me on the lawn. Pink is her favorite color, everything from her canvas shoes to her shorts, t-shirt, and cellphone are pink.

"Caroline, what is happiness to you?"

"Happiness is having fun, when you can do all the stuff you like to do all the time."

"What were some of the happiest moments in your life?"

"Can I mention when somebody else got happy and it made me happy?"

"Absolutely."

"Well, in that case, I was very happy when my brother got accepted to Lehigh University. I was also very happy when my little cousin James was born, and the first time I scored a soccer goal. I still remember I was nine years old, and it made me all teary-eyed."

Mind over matter
Tuesday, 6 April

"Happiness is being able to accept your life with its problems and all. It's being a joyful person, accepting that whatever happens, happens for a reason. Some people say, 'I'll be happy when I get this or that, when I lose a certain amount of pounds.' I don't believe in this: Happiness has to come from inside. It has to be a part of you. It's not an external factor. We ourselves are in charge of our happiness by the way we think and control our emotions. There will be many negative things happening in life but just neglect it, brush it off, and change the energy around you. My grandmother always used to say, 'It's mind over matter: If you don't mind, it doesn't matter.'"

Pinky, a Filipino colleague

My Judaism
Wednesday, 7 April

Five o'clock and still no interview. I must find someone on my way home! I walk slowly through Bryant Park scouting for a suitable "happiness date." A lady in an off-white suit, a beautiful, veiled black hat, glasses, and nice jewelry sits on a chair reading a book.

"Excuse me, may I ask you a question?" I say, and she looks up surprised but also curious and with a kind smile. Her name is Paula.

"My Judaism makes me happy. It gives me a way of life, a sense of self-respect, standards to live up to, and shows me a way of being with people. Do you know what three things have kept the Jewish community together?"

I shake my head.

"We dress differently, speak a different language, and tend to live together." She glances quickly at her watch. "My writing, which gives me an outlet to express myself, is another source of happiness. I write about my community. Sometimes I will also write for ultra-Orthodox publications under a pen name, and I am writing my memoir, which focuses on the transition of going from a traditional Jewish lifestyle to an ultra-Orthodox way of life."

"Are there many differences between the two ways of life?"

"The differences are not as big as with the Pennsylvania Dutch. We have modern commodities at home but most people will not have TV nor will they listen to commercial radio and very often not read the newspapers unless it is for business. Most of our women work in the community, which is a very self-sufficient enclave in Brooklyn. A few of them will work in family-owned jewelry businesses on 47th Street. A small number are lawyers or accountants, mostly working for Orthodox companies. Up until I married my husband 12 years ago, I used to live in Manhattan and led a very different lifestyle. I used to go to the theatres and shows in the city."

"Paula, what was the happiest moment in your life?"

"The happiest moment in my life was definitely the day I got married to my husband 12 years ago. My rabbi had told me he knew somebody he wanted me to meet. He told me he was divorced, with five sons, and that he was born in Israel, where he had been a farmer. I told my rabbi that it wasn't exactly what I was looking for. I rather would have liked a lawyer or an accountant but he reassured me and told me he thought he would be a great match for me. So I went, and it was love at first sight. He makes me so happy."

The privilege of learning
Thursday, 8 April

"I have been thinking about your question, Elisabeth," Chaim, a good friend and colleague from Brazil, tells me. He pushes back some unruly, curly, white hair and adjusts his glasses.

"My intellectual activities make me happy because when I look at a painting, read a book, or listen to music, I put occupations and worries aside. My personal motto is: 'I read in order not to think.' I exist basically in two modes: my reading mode or when I am not reading. Anything that takes me away from thinking makes me happy."

"Isn't this evading reality?"

"For the kind of person I am, thinking does not lead to happiness but to angst. I come from a very intense family. Both my parents were Holocaust survivors and stayed in the German camps. I have also seen a lot of sad things in my professional life. Thinking brings preoccupation and sadness. I rather not think. I basically read or walk."

"You don't think when you walk?"

"The older I get, the more I control my day-dreaming. Now I concentrate on things that are happening right in front of me. I seek to be in tune with nature, with what is going on around me without engaging.

"When I was younger, I needed to be engaged all the time; I wanted to be liked and state my views. Now I am letting it go. I am letting the bone out of my mouth as an old dog should do. I am less anxious, calmer, more in tune, and accepting of what is, rather than what should be. This is illustrated in my attitude toward Gabriel, my autistic son. I still expect him to improve but I accept more that things are the way they are. I continue to try to be a good dad so I can have a clear conscience, even if things turn out in a way I did not plan or hope for."

"Chaim, what were some of the happiest moments in your life?"

"The birth of the kids by far. Everything else will be a distant third.

"The time I spent with my parents as a child. My brother—who was five years older than me and who until today is my best friend—and I grew up in a suburb of Rio de Janeiro full of immigrants: Some of them came from different parts of Brazil but also from different countries. I had a happy childhood, although I was quite insecure as a boy. Since my parents, who were Polish Russians, were immigrants after World War II, I felt I was very different from everybody else. And I was until I realized that this was my individuality. My parents were very supportive. They always told me, 'This is your uniqueness. This is cool.'"

"What are your 'get-happy tricks?'"

"I drink to get tipsy, not drunk, just to a state when I feel lighter and less worried. I read and smoke marijuana."

"My last question to you: Chaim, are you happy?"

"I would not say I am happy. I am content. Happiness is almost bliss. It's the speed of light: It's impossible. It's like Communism: The idea is great but you are never going to get there; it doesn't work. To be content, it's more like socialism. The golden middle way. I am very content that life has given me the privilege of learning."

Always something to be happy about

Friday, 9 April

It has been a sad morning. I have been dealing with administrative issues of a dying friend and colleague. As I sit down on the train going home, a man with a white beard greets me from the other side of the aisle. It gives me the necessary strength to approach him.

"Excuse me, sir, would you mind answering a few questions about happiness?"

"Sure!" He grabs his backpack and sits down next to me.

"What is your definition of happiness?"

"Happiness is to enjoy life regardless of what circumstances you are in. In my later years, I am 63 years old now, I learned that no matter how many problems you face, how many mountaintops you have to climb, there is always something to be happy about. At the end of every day's obstacles, if you tackle it with an open mind and in a right way, there is a reward, which brings you back to happiness.

"Before I used to count down the days of the week for the weekend to arrive but now I try to enjoy every day. Of course, weekends are still nice because I have more time for myself but I don't consider them so much better than the other days of the week because I try to make each day a good day and see the positive in each and every day. You cannot hold grudges nor should you allow anybody to bring you down.

"There is always a reward to being kind. You get kindness back, and this is happiness. You can throw people off guard by being kind to them. During my lunch hour I strive as much as possible to go to the gym. In order to get there, I cross a little square, which is always full of bystanders. As I pass in front of people, I try to get eye contact with them and say, 'Good day.' The younger ones will turn away but people in their 30s and up will usually respond. Older ladies give me their most beautiful smile. This makes me happy."

"What are your tricks to get happy when you are feeling low?"

"When I am feeling sad or depressed, I close my eyes and think of happy places or happy moments. It does not take me long to bring me back to a good mood. I learned a lot when I started studying karate. I was in my 40s and thought I had gained too much weight so my brother-in-law and I enrolled in karate. I started to meditate. Through meditation to happy places, you are cleansed of that ugly feeling of despair and sadness."

"Are you happy?"

"Yes, I am very happy. I have so much to be grateful for. I have had a very good life."

"Where did you grow up?"

"I grew up in a very Italian neighborhood in Brooklyn. My family is from Sicily."

"Just like in *The Godfather*?" I say jokingly.

"Well, this was exactly how I grew up. Let me tell you: The head guy from Long Island in the book *The Godfather,* that was my mother's godfather.

"I remember one time when I was little I went to a girlfriend's house. We were sitting on the floor in her room and chatted. I must have been about 12 years old. All of a sudden I see suitcases under her bed and ask her, 'Why do you keep your clothes under the bed?' She pulled the suitcases from under the bed and opened them. They were full of dollar bills. I asked her, 'Why don't you put it in the bank?' She replied, 'My dad doesn't trust banks.' Later that evening I told this to my mom, and she said, 'Mamma mia, don't you know that her dad is the chief of the mafia around here? This is all dirty money.'

"Another story is the one about her father who had bought some watermelons from the local fruit merchant. In that time there were only a few supermarkets. There was one fish store, one meat store, one egg store, and there was the fruit guy who was selling fruits from his little cart. He had sold her father some watermelons but one of them was no good so he wanted his money back. But the salesman laughed him off and said, 'Don't bother me. Leave me alone.' The wronged customer insisted but once more, the salesman just ignored him. He then returned home, took an axe, searched for the salesman, and cut him up in pieces. The whole neighborhood knew about it but nobody said anything.

"The best story, however, is when my grandmother got robbed. We lived in a three-story house with one aunt on the ground floor, another one on the first floor, and my parents on the second floor. My grandmother lived next door to us. One day my grandmother came running to our house. 'I have been robbed; somebody has stolen my furs, money, diamonds, and my gold.' The police was called but nothing happened. The following day two guys, dressed in impeccable black suits, rang our doorbell. My father recognized them immediately. They belonged to the mob. 'We heard your mother got robbed'—this type of news travelled fast in our neighborhood—'We would like to find those who did it for you,' they told my father. But he did not want to owe them any favors so he quickly said, 'That won't be necessary. I don't want to owe you any favors.' They replied, 'You don't understand, this is on us. Nobody robs our grandmothers.' The next day all the stolen goods were returned to us."

"It was so good to meet you today," I say, "I felt kind of low because a dear friend of mine is dying from cancer."

"I am sorry to hear that. I can identify with what you are telling me because my sister has had lymphoma for four years. She is the mother of my godson. Tomorrow I am going to my godson's wedding. They have postponed their honeymoon so that he can do a bone marrow transplant for his mother. I didn't tell you at the beginning of the interview but if this transplant works and my sister can rid herself of the cancer, then that will be the happiest moment in my life."

Happiness infuses others
Monday, 12 April

I am sitting across the table from Hasan, my colleague from Bangladesh. He has a lot of grey curly hair, and he smiles frequently.

"Hasan, what is your definition of happiness?"

"I don't operate with definitions because they don't work; they change all the time. My motto is: Always be happy because happiness infuses others. When I am happy, I'm more productive, people like me more, and I get more things done. Happiness is infectious. Even when I have problems, I organize myself and compartmentalize them and invest in a more optimistic attitude."

"Can you name one of the happiest moments in your life?"

"The happiest day of my life took place in New York in 2000. The Republicans were going to have their convention in Madison Square Garden. My oldest daughter, Sharmi, had just settled into her school where she became part of a Pro Choice group of boys and girls. They demonstrated in front of the Madison Square Garden, and it turned into an anti-Bush demonstration. She was arrested for 48 hours. After two sleepless nights, I went to court, and they told me that she would not be among those who would be released. When I later called my wife to tell her the news, she said to me, 'Sharmi is here. She has been released.' No other moment could ever compare to that moment of pure joy that I experienced that day."

"What are your happiness tricks?"

"I once read a very good book about happiness from Burton Russell called *The Conquest of Happiness*. There I saw this quote that said, 'The only way you can conquer happiness is if you can create an inner world within yourself.' I literally do it: Even if I am in a crowd, I can withdraw inside myself and separate myself from the crowd. What helps me in my darkest moments is my faith in my kids, my wife, my books, my writing, my music, and soon to be gardening. Since I am an atheist, I do not have a god to fall back on so I fall back on my godly things, and those are my godly things.

"Even in my darkest hour, I can find something to cheer me up: my assignments. I always have an assignment: Every week I need to produce a 1500-word article for a Bengali magazine. Whenever I am sad, I deliberately push myself into tomorrow's articles. I go from my real life to my imagined life.

"I remember one evening, many years ago, I went to a bar with two friends: one poet and one painter. They were both pretty drunk. The painter said something nasty but the poet only answered, 'This night will end, and the sun will rise, and there is nothing you can do about it.' This is true: The night will end, and the sun will rise, all things good and bad will eventually come to an end.

"People expect too much from their own lives, Elisabeth, such as promotions, friends, and marriage. The higher the expectations, the bigger the disappointments. I am a human being with low expectations. For me, this life is Heaven and Hell. I look for Heaven in the smallest things—the sunrise, the rain, the blooming of the flowers. The most remarkable thing is watching my daughter grow. Every single day I live through them, and I become younger. Hopefully, if they can take a little bit of me, when I die I will remain with them."

Making love
Tuesday, 13 April

"What is so funny?"

I am sitting in Sharon's office. We have known each other for a long time and always get the giggles when we are together.

"Oh, it's nothing," she chuckles. "I can't believe this is the first thing that comes to my mind when you ask about happiness. I cannot say it."

I look at her pleadingly.

"Ok, then, to make love, not sex, is one of my favorite things to do in life. I would do it ten times a day if I could. My last boyfriend was good in that respect."

We laugh wickedly.

"The second thing that makes me happy is money. I wouldn't want it to buy pretty things but to get freedom to be myself, to have peace of mind, to free me from working to get medical benefits, and allow me to do things that I really want to do such as going to a friend's wedding in Ecuador."

"What are your happiness tricks?"

She covers her mouth, blushes, and laughs. "I must be the horniest girl in the world but making love makes me happy.

"The things that sustain me for longer periods of time could be reading a good book, drinking water, doing yoga, or random acts of kindness.

"If I were an enlightened being, just being present in the now would probably be enough to make me happy again. But I am very aware of my health, which is not too good, so it might make me more depressed. Sometimes I think we rob ourselves of being."

What doesn't kill you
makes you stronger
Thursday, 22 April

I am having lunch with Ahmad, one of my colleagues. His voice is deep, powerful, and melodious.

"As you know, I am from Egypt," he says, "and we grow up being taught about God and using the expression '*Insha Allah*' (God willing) all the time. But as I get older, I have lost some of my childhood beliefs. I believe in destiny, that what is meant to be is meant to be. In my younger years I would always have lots of regrets if things didn't work out the way I wanted. But now I have acquired acceptance for what is, and if something does not go through, I think it wasn't meant to be, and that something better will come along. But at the same time I do believe that you create your own happiness and your own destiny. If you wish for something hard enough, you can make it happen.

"In my career I have also lived countless happy, tragic, and dramatic moments. I remember the year 1989 when the Berlin Wall fell. At that time I was the Middle East Bureau Chief for Reuters TV (formerly known as Visnews) based in Cairo. But when the Wall fell, I was sent to Prague, where I set up the Eastern European Bureau. It was an amazing time: Just like a house of cards tumbling down, the former allies of the Soviet Union started collapsing one by one: Romania, Bulgaria, Hungary, Poland. I witnessed the Velvet Revolution in Czechoslovakia and Vaclav Havel coming to power.

"Then in August 1990 Saddam Hussein invaded Kuwait, and I was sent to Saudi Arabia to set up the Reuters TV news operation there. In February 1991, when the allied troops liberated Kuwait, our teams accompanied the troops as they crossed the border from Saudi Arabia into Kuwait after the air war. In August 1991 I returned to my post in London. No sooner had I returned when I found myself being posted in New York as News Operations Manager in the Reuters TV Bureau. In late 1992 the then Secretary General of the United Nations Boutros Boutros-Ghali offered me the position of Deputy Spokesperson to the Secretary General. This was also a very proud and happy moment in my life."

"Ahmad, what are your tricks to make yourself happy?"

"Grief never stays with me for a long time. The only time I was sad for a long, long time was in August 2003 when Islamic terrorists bombed the UN Headquarters in Baghdad, known as Canal Hotel. The Special Representative of the Secretary-General, my friend and former boss Sergio Vieira de Mello, and my dear, dear friend Nadia Younes were killed, with 20 other colleagues. You see, not only did the UN lose 22 wonderful civil servants but I lost many close friends in that coward attack. The ensuing year was terribly hard for me.

"I can anger quite quickly and become very upset for five minutes. I count to ten, take a deep breath, try to calm myself down, and say to myself, 'If it didn't kill me, it made me stronger.' A few years ago I was on my deathbed. There was a 50 per cent chance of living or dying, due to the accumulation of stress, but by some miracle I made it. After that, I realized that one has to achieve a work-life balance; nothing at work is worth losing one's life over. We must appreciate what we have and move on."

Happiness is life itself
Thursday, 29 April

As I glance up from my desk, I notice my colleague Franck from Togo standing at the copying machine. This is my chance!

"Can you name some things that make you happy?"

"Friendship. It's the simplest form of all relationships. It relates to the basic human need of being in a relationship to a fellow human being. True friendship, the idea that you can be there for somebody and that they will be there for you, is comforting. The simple fact of it existing makes me very happy.

"The fact of coming, going, moving around, being active in contrast to inertia, makes me happy. Life gives me an opportunity to be able to enjoy little things every day: laughing with somebody, having a good time with a colleague, basically, feeling alive. Happiness is life itself. I dream of being alive every day: cry if I need to cry, laugh when I want to laugh, be quiet or loud when I feel like it."

"What is happiness?"

"It's the realization that as a human being you have the freedom of being, and that you can be who and what you want. If you know that you can be who and what you are, then there is no reason not to be happy."

"Do you think that we all can be what we want and who we are?"

"Yes, we all can but we often give up too early on what we can or want to be. Sometimes we fall victims of circumstances and let that take over our lives. There is a long way between knowing what and who you are and want to be, and being who and what you want to be. For me, just knowing it gives me a reason to be happy. When there is a will, there is a way. We were all born to be free—by freedom I here mean the ability to do and not to do—and this is the greatest gift of all. Using my freedom wisely is my way of trying to be who and what I want to be."

My Indian wedding
Friday, 30 April

Since morning, my husband and I have been running around trying to finalize the last-minute shopping for his transfer to Japan. In all this, I have not had time for a "happiness date." I am therefore thrilled when Pascal, one of the guests at the farewell dinner, accepts to answer my questions. He is from Brittany, has lots of white hair, and a large mustache that curves up at each end.

"Pascal, what is happiness to you?"

"At my age happiness is serenity and peace."

"What were some of the happiest moments in your life?"

"7 November 1993 at 7:15 a.m. when I pulled out Nevenn from my wife's womb. You see, in France, once the head and the shoulders have passed the uterus, one is allowed to pull out the baby. This was an amazing moment, plus a few minutes later when Nevenn peed on the nurse!" He laughs humorously.

"When I got married to Uju in Bombay, India, in 1991, it was held in a hotel that was right on the beach with 500 guests. It was amazing to be there with my wife and all her relatives and see the camels walking on the beach. It was a totally disconcerting experience for this little boy from Brittany.

"A third event that really marked me was when Nevenn was eight and a half months old and I had gone for a one month's business trip to France. When I came home, I was so scared that he would have forgotten about me. But when he saw me, he reached out his arms and gave me an enormous smile. I totally melted."

May

My kids
Wednesday, 5 May

A friend and I are taking the train home together. He seems somber. It is time to make him focus on the happier things in his life.

"Tell me three things that make you happy."

"When there is harmony at home, when husband and wife act lovingly and respectfully toward each other, and the kids are doing well in school. A good way to find out if a couple is still in love is if they hold hands or if there is a gleam in their eyes when they look at each other at a party. In my house, this is very rare: maybe a couple of days in a year."

My friend stares straight ahead, and I observe his handsome profile against the window.

"Good health. When you have no health problems, happiness is there. When you are healthy, you can do what you want to do. For example, my favorite foods are hamburgers, subway sandwiches, and pizza. I remember when I was younger, together with two friends, we would order six feet of subway sandwiches and literally stuff our faces. After finishing those, we would hardly be able to move but we were so happy!" He reminisces nostalgically. "These days, due to my cholesterol, I eat half a one-footer!

"Help others. Everybody has skills, and when I can use whatever skills I have to assist others, this makes me really happy. I don't expect anything back. Helping is, in itself, a source of self-satisfaction."

"What were some of the happiest moments in your life?"

A big smile suddenly illuminates his face.

"When my daughter Anna was born, I was so happy I cried. I usually never cry. Just to see that little creature and that she depended on me was something amazing. Other happy moments are when I come home at night and both my kids—they are ten and eight years old—run to greet me. They usually sing a silly song, hug me for a good while, and then they run away.

"A wonderful time of the day is also bedtime. First, the three of us go to my daughter's room, and we sit on her bed while I read them a bedtime story. Then, I tell my son to go to his room, and my daughter and I chitchat a little bit. I ask her, 'So what was new about school today?' Her standard answer, which I am sure so many parents can identify with, is always 'Nothing, nothing.' Although I already know the answer, I keep asking every night because maybe, just maybe, if one day there were any problems, maybe she would tell me. I want them to know I am asking. After tucking her in, I go to my son's room. We usually shoot some hoops, then I put him to bed. My kids are so funny; when I hug them before they go to bed, they won't let go of me so I tickle them until they take their arms off me.

"Finally, a major happy moment was when I got my BMW. I had ordered it, and it took six months in arriving. I remember I was at work that day; when I got the call in the office, I screamed of joy. The salesperson, who was not supposed to be working the following day when I was going to pick up the car, said to me, 'I had to come in on my day off to see that smile on your face!' When I drove my new car to the office the following morning, all my colleagues were waiting for me in the parking lot."

"My last question: Are you happy?"

"The only thing that makes me unhappy is the wife. What would make me truly happy would be to find my soulmate, who would accept me for who I really am."

When I became a Consecrated Virgin

Thursday, 6 May

"Elisabeth, are you free for lunch today?" a former colleague of mine calls to ask.

Three hours later I meet up with her at a nearby restaurant. She is wearing jeans, a grey t-shirt, and a wooden cross around her neck. She has thick, short, salt-and-pepper hair, a nice brown tan, lively brown eyes, and laughs easily. We chat for a long time about life, its joys and challenges. Then she directs the conversation toward my happiness project.

"The first thing that makes me happy is Our Lady. Jesus was God and man but Our Lady was from our side of the world, earth side. You can expect from her all sympathy and understanding without saying too much. She knows all."

"Have you ever seen the Virgin Mary?"

"Yes, Elisabeth, I have. After having been evacuated from Zambia where I had been ambushed by some men—it was a traumatic experience—I returned to New York City. My apartment was right in front of the Nigerian mission to the United Nations. For several years I would see the contour of Our Lady reflected in the windows of the Nigerian mission. I even asked some colleagues to come and look at it. Some saw her, others didn't, but I kept seeing her for some seven years. I think she wanted to console me.

"The second thing that makes me happy is the Blessed Sacrament. Our Lord Jesus in his earthly life spoke about his body and blood. In the Last Supper, as a memorial, he commanded that it should be celebrated and whoever ate the bread and drank the wine would carry Jesus in himself and attain salvation. Each time we eat the consecrated bread and drink the consecrated wine the cells in our body change. You are laying a signpost in Heaven so when your soul separates from your body, your signpost will remind you that you received the blood and body of Jesus, who paved the way for you to have eternal life.

"The third thing that makes me happy is the unity of nations. There is no place like the United Nations. It's a house of peace. I was working on the council for an independent Namibia for several years, and the fact that we were able to get all the fighting factions together around the table, and initiate a dialogue, was a tremendous occurrence. Sometimes we would go one step forward and two steps back but the United Nations is the only place where you can look into the eyes of your enemy and still talk."

"Would you mind sharing some of the happiest moments in your life?" I ask her.

"The independence of Namibia in 1990. I had worked on it for 14 years as a political affairs officer. When Namibia finally got its independence, I felt as if I had been running a race and just crossed the finishing line. After the independence, I travelled with the Council for Namibia of the United Nations to hand over the keys of independence to the President of Namibia. This was an amazing experience.

"Another extremely happy moment was when I thought Palestine would obtain its independence in 1997-1998. During my last years at the United Nations, I was the Chief of the Palestine and Decolonization Unit.

"Finally, one of the happiest moments in my life was when I became a Consecrated Virgin. Consecrated Virgins are professional women who give their lives to Christ. It took place in St. John the Baptist Church. My dress was made in Fatima, in Portugal. My ceinture had a painting of the vision that Sister Lucia—one of the shepherd girls to whom the Virgin appeared in Portugal—had had of the Blessed Virgin and the Holy Trinity. My cape was made out of linen and embroidered with all the flags of the United Nations, which had been sown on it by Palestinian women in Gaza. Seven gold bangles given to me by my mother decorated my wrists, and I also had two beautiful Indian silk carpets from Kashmir. It was the bishop who consecrated me while I lay prostrate before the altar. When they sang the litany of the saints, I offered myself to God, with all the nations of the world, and all the staff who work for the United Nations. All my colleagues were there. After the consecration, we had a small reception with very good wine that we got from the Portuguese mission. There was also a band of native Indians playing music from the Andes, whom I had heard on the platform one day as I was waiting for the subway. I had asked them if they wished to play on my consecration day, and they accepted. This made it very special."

Acceptance
Saturday, 8 May

The cell phone next to my bed rings.

"Hi, this is Walt. Are you still available for coffee this morning?"

I suddenly am wide awake. "Absolutely! Is 9:15 good?"

I leap out of bed, shower, and speed over to the supermarket where we have agreed to meet. Walt is around 65 years old, slender, with white hair, blue eyes, and a wonderful smile. He is wearing jeans and a Rutgers polo shirt with large red and blue stripes.

We sit down in the cafe overlooking the store. There is something soothing about seeing staff preparing sandwiches, Japanese chefs prepping sushi at their station, and bakers busying themselves behind baskets of baguettes, a wide selection of pastries, bagels, and muffins.

"I have been trying to think about what you asked me. One thing that certainly makes me happy is to accomplish something I set out to do that was a challenge. You see, when I was a child, my life was all about survival. When I grew up to be a teenager, I said to myself, 'Why should I challenge myself? Just go and find a safe place to work.' I became a pipe fitter but after 25 years, I started feeling bored. When I was 48 years old, I saw a course on self-hypnosis, which promised to find a way to relax and to improve concentration. Just what I needed! I took the course and became very good at it. Do you know that I have actually had teeth pulled and had root canals done without anesthesia?"

I gasp.

"Even the doctor was amazed. One day one of my teachers asked me if I could step in for him and teach. I decided to challenge myself. Whatever opportunities I would get, I would take them. The first day I taught a class, my knees were shaking. I kept teaching for many years. I even started a part-time business with self-hypnosis. It gave me confidence. Every time I challenged myself, I felt better about myself. After a while I just quit my plumbing job with its security, seniority, vacations, and other benefits."

"Walt, what is your definition of happiness?"

"I don't think there is such a thing called happiness. I think it's a temporary emotional state based on feeling emotionally safe, rewarded, and excited. Happiness is an individual experience. Look at skydivers, who challenge themselves in dangerous ways. To one person, this would be a nightmare but for those who do this, it is a near bliss experience.

"I don't think that life is so much about happiness but rather about how to live your life. I think that life is great if you know how to play it by its games and rules."

"What do you mean by that, Walter?"

"There is no one book that has the answers on how to live your life well. A lot of it depends on each human being's circumstances. I think it is very important not to see challenges as 'poor me's but as opportunities of growth. This way you have influence over your life. Life is about working, not about getting our way. When we work at it, we will get rewards.

"Finally, part of learning to live is an opportunity to learn how to manage not getting our way. Sometimes we have to not get our way. Acceptance is the answer to all our problems today. If there is a person, event, thing, or situation that is troubling me, it is because I am not accepting that person, event, thing, or situation as being exactly as it should be today. Nothing, absolutely nothing, occurs in God's world by mistake. I can only be happy when I accept life on life's terms. Every difficult situation in my life is a challenge for me to create an opportunity for my personal growth. My happiness is the result of the change that I make within me and my attitudes."

I love listening to his words. The store is now buzzing with customers, and we are on our second cup of coffee.

"What are your happiness tricks?"

"I can't be happy when I am down. We are really grieving quite often: death, relationships dissolving, problems that loved ones are encountering. We also grieve unfulfilled expectations. We would need to be a robot not to feel sad. It is healthy to grieve, and we have to allow ourselves to go through a grieving process. I actually developed a process similar to my pain management technique that can turn a grieving process into a state of euphoria. I relax instead of getting tense. I move from sadness into a state of lightness.

"My father died in 2005. The first Christmas without him was very difficult. In our house this holiday was always a very big celebration. I remember the firetruck coming by with candy canes, and I started feeling very emotional. I lay down in the recliner, started to relax, and focused on my body instead of why I was sad, accepting without getting all the thoughts such as 'I wish he was here.' It healed what I experienced at that moment, although I still had more grieving to do. I felt a lightness, a spiritual feeling that was incredible.

"If you are unhappy, check the way you think. Your intellect should be talking to your emotional state. Everybody has a six-year-old emotional state—getting your way, selfish—in them, which is about survival. We are born with this. Our growth process is all about moving from the emotional state into an intellectual one. We need emotion to have fun but we need our intellect to make important decisions. We need to teach the six-year-old that getting our way is not the answer. We need to teach patience and understanding. It's all part of coping with life.

"Our perception of life is based on the way we are describing it. If you wouldn't say it to a six-year-old, don't say it to yourself either. Once you get used to this, your life gets easier. Let's take an example: You get up, and today is the day you have planned a picnic but it's raining. Your six-year-old self might get all emotional and say, 'Why is it raining?' and feel all upset. Instead, try to talk to your adult self: 'This is not helping. Let's postpone it to another day or let's go to the museum instead.'

"Acceptance will steer you in a direction you never chose on your own and will give you new opportunities you never knew existed. It doesn't mean you have to accept any situation. Each day you are dealt a hand, and that's the one you have to play. Some people are dealt a terrible hand, and they can still turn it into a winning game. When you are working on self-improvement, life is like an adventure. Maturity is about seeing the whole picture in comparison with only that of the six-year-old. Growth is moving from infancy level to disciplining our emotional freedom.

"You have to see life as an opportunity, not as a guarantee for rewards. Life is fair: We get what we need."

The day I got married

Sunday, 9 May

"A very happy moment in my life was the day I got married. It was a big hurdle because my dad did not talk to me for three years. You see, I was born and raised in Kenya by Indian parents. When I was 14 years old, we moved to London. Although my parents had lived outside of India for many, many years, by the time I was in my mid-20s my father had still not changed his rigid way of thinking. He was of the opinion that I should marry somebody from my caste. But I had already found the man I loved and fought to have the right to marry him for three years. My father's older brothers stood by me as well. It helped that my husband was also a vegetarian, had the same belief system, and spoke the same language as me. Finally, my father gave in, and once he met my husband, he accepted him and grew very fond of him."

Devyani, a soccer mom

When my son graduated from Yale
Thursday, 13 May

"Excuuuuuuuuuuuuuuuuuuuuuuuuuuuse me!" I run after Sandra, the cleaning lady in our building, who is just exiting the restroom.

"May I ask you some questions about happiness, please?"

"Why you want that?" she replies with a Puerto Rican accent.

After I explain my project to her, she agrees.

"I like to spend time with my son and my husband." She seems to have run out of things to say.

"Are there other things that make you happy, Sandra?"

"I am a very simple person. I am usually happy and appreciate when I can go to and from work without any problems, and when there are no problems at work.

"My mother makes me very happy. She is an extremely sweet person. She is a strong believer and prays a lot. Whenever I have a problem, she always comforts me; she gives me strength and faith that everything will be ok."

"Tell me some of the happiest moments in your life, Sandra."

"One of the happiest days in my life was my wedding day in Puerto Rico in 1978. We had a wonderful big celebration with friends and family.

"Another happy moment was when my son was born 27 years ago, when he finished high school and was accepted at NYU, Columbia, Cornell, Penn University, and Yale, and finally in 2004 when he graduated in History from Yale together with President Bush's daughter. This was a very proud and happy moment in my life."

Windows of love
Saturday, 15 May

"Some of the happiest moments in my life were when my children were born. When I had my first child, it was like a window of love that I did not know existed opened in my heart. When I got my second baby, I never imagined that yet another window could open in my heart. It was magical. I especially got this feeling with the two first children since the feeling was so new. With my last child, I was so afraid that the third window would close because she had sleep apnea and I was so scared that she would die. I hardly slept the first year she was born."

Marcela, Chilean friend

A beach without jellyfish and crabs
Saturday, 22 May

My Chilean friend Marcela and her family have invited my son and me to join them at the beach. Our sons are playing lacrosse and Camila, my friend's 11-year-old daughter, and I are wading in the water collecting seashells. When we take a break to drink some lemonade, I interview Camila. She still has a round, childlike face, and when she speaks, you see her braces. She is wearing a striped cotton sundress.

"Camila, what three things make you happy?"

"Reading. I've started a new book called *Molly Moon's Incredible Book of Hypnotism*. It's really good. It's about this little girl who lived in an orphanage. They had found her in a box. She hates the orphanage because the people are mean to her. One day she goes to the library where she finds a book about hypnotism and takes it home. And this is how far I have read…"

Her eyes shine excitedly. "Going on the swing set in the backyard—I do that every day once I have finished my homework—and spending time with friends and family. I have a lot of friends. We bike to the pool, go swimming. In winter, we sled behind my best friend's backyard."

"Camila, what are some of the happiest moments in your life?"

"The day I found out my friend was taking me to Disney World. It took us two days to drive there. We had such a fun time and went on many rides. Although I was scared sometimes, we still had a great vacation. My trips arriving in Chile every year for vacation are also happy moments in my life, and when we got our dog Bongo."

"I have one more question for you: Are you happy?"

She gives me a big smile and pulls at her striped sundress. "Yes because I am going to the beach. I don't like jellyfish and crabs though!"

The year my parents retired
Monday, 24 May

"Excuse me, may I ask you a question?"

A girl with long brown hair who is sitting by herself at a table at Barnes & Noble looks up. Heeyun is from Korea. "Hee" means 'happy' and "yun" means "truth." What a wonderful name!

"What is your definition of happiness?"

A flicker of sadness crosses her young face.

"To me, happiness would be to be reunited with my parents and my younger sister in Korea. I live alone here, and I miss them."

"Tell me some of the happiest moments in your life."

"Well, one of the happiest periods was my last year in Korea. Since I was born, both my parents worked very hard and had little time for me. But that year they stopped working to spend more time with us, and it was wonderful. We didn't do anything special: We just spent time together. Sometimes we would go for walks in some nearby mountains.

"Another thing that made me very happy was when I was eight years old and got a little sister and lastly, when I first arrived in New York in January to learn English. I found the city with its diverse cultures and my newfound freedom very exciting."

"Is life in Korea very different from life in New York?"

"Yes, for instance, when you go to a restaurant here in New York, everybody takes their own plate; in Korea, we share all our dishes. Also here there are taxes and tips on the bill in the restaurant but not in Korea.

"People in the U.S. are very friendly. When they see you, they will wave at you and say 'hi.' It's very different in Korea. The first time I meet somebody my age or younger I will bow, then I can wave at them and say 'hi.' Whenever I meet someone older than me, I should always bow, and when I speak with them, I should not maintain eye contact. To look them straight in the eyes or to wave at them would be very rude."

"What do you do to get happy again when you are feeling down?"

"When I feel depressed, I rest at home, sleep, and listen to Korean ballads or I walk around town by myself."

Body piercing
Saturday, 29 May

I notice him immediately as I enter the café, dressed entirely in black with dark blond hair and a goatee. It wasn't his garments that attracted me but the piercings and the tattoos. In each of his ear lobes he has huge black plugs and in one tragus a blue stud. Large tattoos cover his arms, and his open shirt lets me catch a glimpse of some drawings on his chest. A labret pierces his chin, and later when he speaks I discover that his tongue is pierced. His name is Chuck.

"My job as a body piercer makes me very happy. After high school I started working for a company but hated all the office politics. It was like it was high school all over again. Five years ago I started my own piercing company because I wanted to be in charge."

"I don't know so much about body piercing. Is there a philosophy behind it?"

"There are a lot of different philosophies behind piercing. First, you have the neo tribalism movement: They are the ones who want a return to the tribal past. Here in this country, for instance, you had the Nez Perce Indians who pierced their nose or the Eskimos who pierce their lips. There are also the futurists who view the body as a machine and try to push the limits of what can be done in terms of modifying and changing it. The sado-masochists view pain as an end in itself, and finally, you have those who just want to embellish their bodies."

He opens up his short-sleeved shirt and shows me some sun-looking tattoos on his right chest and shoulder.

"Look here! They are spheres of light from the islands of Borneo. The tribes who make these tattoos believe that our afterlives are a photo-negative of this life. So the darker the tattoos, the brighter they will shine in the afterlife."

Tolerance
Sunday, 30 May

"Hi, Elisabeth!"

My friend Linda opens the door. Ghassan, her husband, is right behind her. He is of medium height, wears glasses, has a tanned complexion, and has thick, short, white hair. I interview him while my friend prepares dinner.

"What makes you happy?"

"To see my family really happy, to know that my work and effort over the years have made a difference in their lives, that they are on the right path, and to see that they have loving thoughts toward us and the rest of the world." He pauses, then adds, "sometimes I think I have failed but then my wife says, 'No, you didn't, it's momentary.' It makes me happy to see them successful. My role as a father is to help them reach their potential."

His voice is kind and soft and infused with a heavy Arabic accent. He reflects for a while before continuing. "Seeing acceptance in other people of whom I am and where I come from"—he is from Palestine—"to see tolerance, to be looked at as a human being, and not to be stereotyped as a group. I truly believe that regardless of where we are from, our religion or the color of our skin, as human beings we share common elements: love and peace. We should steer away from pride and ego because it creates differences in people."

"What were some of the happiest moments in your life?"

"Besides being with my wife and kids, whenever I think of happiness I think about my childhood. It was wonderful. We were four brothers and seven sisters. I am the youngest. Three of my sisters never married and still live in our home. Whenever I call them, I feel the same love coming through the telephone as they ask me: 'What did you eat today?' or 'How are you feeling today?' It's like my mother is still there. She was an amazing person. She was 16 when she married my father, who was 42 years old. I was 14 when she encouraged me to leave so I did. First to Kuwait, then to Germany. I didn't understand why she wanted me to leave the family but I later understood as she told me, 'I didn't want the military to come and take you.' Except for two times that she came to visit me in the United States, I didn't see her for 26 years.

"When I left Palestine, I was a teenager. I returned as a grown man with a wife and three children. When my mother greeted me in her home after those 26 years, she started singing a song containing three of four phrases about how happy she was."

June

When I met my daughter

Wednesday, 2 June

Sophie, my French colleague, and I are having lunch in her cubicle as we are chatting about happiness.

"One of the happiest moments in my life was when I met my daughter Annabelle for the first time," she says. "We had placed an ad in the newspaper, if there was a young mother who would let us adopt her baby at birth. First, we had to find out what states authorized such ads because this is not permitted everywhere. In August we got a reply from a grandmother of a little baby who would be born in February. It was the grandmother who had seen our ad because her daughter (the mom) was only 16 years old. We started communicating with the young mother every week to let her know that it was a very generous act from her side to want the best for her daughter, and a smart move so she herself could return to school. We wanted the mother to trust us and to know that the baby would be well taken care of with us. At the same time we did not want to invest ourselves too much either: What if the mother changed her mind after her baby was born and wanted to keep it? In February we got a text message informing us of the birth of the baby. We booked our tickets but, due to a snowstorm, we had to wait four days before we could get there. We got to the hospital to the nursing station and…" Sophie's voice trails off as she starts to cry. "I recall seeing her in her little bed. She weighed over seven pounds and had light brown hair and blue eyes. She was so beautiful."

Aloneness

Friday, 4 June

My friend Gill and I are sitting on a bench in the shade of some large trees in a quiet corner of a park.

"Tell me some things that make you happy."

"Being somewhere quiet and beautiful where I can listen to the birdsong, a place with real tranquility for the soul. I am very affected by my surroundings: The hardest thing about living in New York is the noise level, the amount of people everywhere. I find it claustrophobic. I need to spend time alone—that's when I find the most happiness. In all the other places I have lived, I always had easy access to the countryside. When we lived in France, for example, I would take the dog and walk for hours in the vineyards, and I would sing and cry—in short, do whatever I wanted."

"Where do you find this time and space alone now?"

"As you know, we live on Roosevelt Island. My favorite spot used to be the tip of the island. Before it was completely wild, and I would sit down on a large rock and watch as the ocean came in on one side of the island and the East River on the other. The crickets would be chirping, and the cormorants would dive for fish in the river. Sometimes I would go and sit there after work or after breakfast on the weekends. I would bring my coffee and just feel the peace come over me. I call it soul food: Your soul is fed by beauty and tranquility."

Maybe it is all this walking under blue skies along clear oceans that has created the beautiful blue color of her eyes. Gill is 55 years old but looks much younger. Today she is wearing brown pants, nice brown shoes, a khaki top, and a floral linen sweater. Sunglasses hold back her blond hair.

"Another source of happiness is spending time with my daughters, one is 16 years old and the other one is 18. We hang out in their bedrooms and chat. We are very close and talk a lot."

"Gill, tell me some of the happiest moments in your life."

"Getting married to Juan. It lasted for a long weekend. We got married in a small village on the northern coast of Spain called Santillana del Mar. I had arranged for 20 of my friends from the United Kingdom to come; otherwise, my parents were the only ones from my family to attend. The rest of the guests were Juan's family.

The wedding ceremony took place in a small 12th century church. The reception followed in a parador of the village. The next day we all had paella in a restaurant near the beach. It was a warm and very loving environment.

"You asked me for another happy moment in my life. I would say that it is more about a period of my life. We had some wonderful years when we bought our first house on the coast between Valencia and Alicante. It was a 200-year-old house made of stone. I came up with new designs, and together we remodeled it. I loved smelling the jasmine trees in the evening, the pine trees at dawn. In the morning the swallows would dive after the flies over the swimming pool. I loved the feel of warm air and sun. Then you had the changing colors of the Mediterranean and the sky. Our daughters were 5 and 7 at the time, not difficult teenagers. Our relationship was great. We created what we thought would be our corner of paradise. I was filled with hope and excitement for the future."

"Are you happy?"

"I would say overall 'yes.' I have travelled extensively and seen so much misery that I have learnt to try to find happiness wherever I am."

Happiness is health
Saturday, 5 June

"Happiness is being healthy. As long as we are healthy, I am happy. When my son was three years old, they found a tumor in his brain. He had been acting funny and losing his coordination. It was affecting his spine. His first surgery lasted 13 hours. I will never forget when they put him on the gurney and wheeled him away. I had asked if I could be there for the surgery but they strongly dissuaded me from attending. I was pregnant at the time. The next day they did an MRI to see if they had been able to remove all the malignant cells but they discovered that there were more tumors in the tissues. They had to perform a new operation on him. This one lasted eight hours. After the surgery he went for chemotherapy for 18 months: He lost all his hair after the first session. I slept at the hospital every night for several months. It was so sad to see kids who did not get many visitors; probably their parents were single parents and had to work. I was lucky to be with him.

"This whole experience gave me a new perspective: I worry less, especially over little tedious things such as bickering in the family and in the office. We really have to count our blessings when we are healthy."

Jennie, a soccer mom

Our farm

Sunday, 6 June

Buttercup is grazing peacefully in the field behind us. She is a large white pony whose age is anywhere between 25 and 30 years old, and she lives on the farm on our street. I am sitting on the grass with Lori and her two-month-old twins while her husband is working on the vegetable beds.

"Tell me three things that make you happy, Lori."

"Our farm. It has been in my husband's family for five generations, and being able to continue the work on this farm makes me very happy." She smiles. "Our new family. Our twin girls are now ten weeks old. We are over the moon about them. And finally, our own food. We have created a Community Supported Agriculture, which is a project in which people buy shares ahead of time. Every week, between June to October, every shareholder will get vegetables. Through this system shareholders partake in the ups and downs of farming. We have a wide selection of vegetables—they are all organic—such as peppers, eggplants, basil, cilantro, parsley, yellow and green zucchini, different types of tomatoes, lettuce, beets, carrots, broccoli, cauliflower, cabbage, green beans, sweet potatoes, and potatoes, and also flowers. We also have half a dozen chickens, a black Labrador, and a cranky old barn cat."

"What are your tricks when you are feeling down or upset to get happy again, Lori?"

"We enjoy working in the garden, cooking for somebody, and sharing that together."

The way I am
Wednesday, 9 June

How my borough of Queens has changed!

I have a wedding to attend in Spain in two weeks so I return to my old neighborhood to have Elisabeth, my Colombian hairdresser, do my hair. As she wraps my hair in foil paper, I seize the moment to interview her.

"What makes me very happy is that my husband takes so good care of me. He is always loving me, talking to me, making a lot of jokes. In short, he makes me feel good about myself. It was a friend of mine who introduced us to each other. One day he told me, 'We have the perfect man for you!' They decided to invite us both for dinner. The day came, and I grew increasingly nervous and called to cancel. I did not want to bother with a relationship at that time. I told them I was running late and that my car had broken down but it didn't stop them. So they sent a car for me, and I really didn't have much of a choice but to go. That was pretty much it. We felt instantaneous attraction for each other and got along very well. Eight months later he proposed to me, and on 19 November 2009, we got married. I am 56 years old, and he is 49 but it doesn't matter." She pauses.

"The second thing that makes me happy is the way I am. Every day I wake up happy with lots of energy. I enjoy cooking for my family and making my partner happy. I love to joke. I also love my job. I used to live in a village called Buenaventura on the coast of Colombia. When I was 15 years old my parents bought me a hairdresser salon, where I started working after having studied hair cutting at school for a year and got my own clients. I worked for four years but until the day I got married I never managed the money. That was my mother's job. When I married my husband at the age of 21, I got a regular paycheck. I worked in that salon until I was approximately 39 years old when I wanted to try my luck in the States and moved to New York. I first worked in a printing factory for four and a half years until I was able to get my hairdresser license. Once I obtained that, I started my own salon in Roosevelt in Queens, which I had for six years until I bought this one, which I sold after 15 years."

It is raining heavily outside, and raindrops are rebounding from the pavement as they pummel the ground. Umbrellas of all colors hurry by, some of the passers-by glancing inside the store. Latin rhythms are playing smoothly in the background. From the walls black and white portraits of Marilyn Monroe, Audrey Hepburn, and James Dean are staring back at me. Under the picture of the latter a text reads: "Dream as if you will live forever, live as if you will die today." Nice motto to live by! I wake up from my reverie.

"What is your definition of happiness?"

"Happiness is a feeling you get when you do good things for other people without being asked to do so, whether it be friends, family, or random people that you encounter in your life. I have always liked to share what I have."

It is now or never
Thursday, 10 June

"What were some of the happiest moments in your life?"

Osvaldo, a colleague from Colombia, is sitting in a blue chair in my office.

"I have so many happy moments, especially now. I just find reasons to be happy. During the last 15 years of my life—I just turned 50—I realized that there is no need to have a perfect job or to live in a perfect city: All is artificial. Happiness comes from within. I became truly happy the day I stopped looking for happiness outside of me and instead focused on the inside.

"If many people are not happy, it's either because they look for happiness outside of themselves or because they are not satisfied due to ungratefulness for what they have. Hopefully, with age comes wisdom.

"Happiness is living and being able to be satisfied with the present moment. It's a state of mind, an attitude. It is now or never. Do what makes you happy!"

Padre Pio

Saturday, 12 June

At last I have arrived! Sitting on a low hill overlooking farms, forests, and surrounded by fields is the Padre Pio Center. The chapel was built as a replica of Our Lady of Grace Church in San Giovanni Rotondo, Italy, where Padre Pio had been a priest. He never came here but Vera Calandra, a devout Catholic, built it in his honor after Padre Pio performed a miracle on her daughter, Vera Marie.

A priest is walking down the aisle of the chapel.

"Good morning, Father. What is under glass there inside the confessional?"

"That is one of the gloves that Padre Pio used to wear. You see, he had stigmata and bled from his forehead, his back, and his hands, just like Jesus did when they crucified him. In order not to get the blood everywhere, he would wear gloves. This confessional was brought here from Italy. Padre Pio really believed in the power of confession, and very often he would sit inside this confessional for 18 hours a day."

I sit down on the first row of the chapel and pray. A deep peace and a strong sense of God enter my whole being. I keep looking at the altar. Suddenly, an Italian-looking lady with short black hair and a navy-blue flowered skirt slightly covered by a light blue apron appears. She glances quickly at the rows of benches in the chapel. I am sitting very close to her.

"Excuse me, miss. Would you by any chance be one of Vera's sisters?"

The priest had told me that one of Vera Marie's sisters is working in the center.

"Yes, I am Julia, her oldest sister."

She has big beautiful brown eyes. With a trembling voice I ask if I can interview her. She agrees, sits down on the front row of the church, and starts telling her story.

"I was the first daughter of my parents. We were six siblings: Michael, me, Francesca, Maria, Vera Marie, and Christina. At the time when Padre Pio performed this miracle, I was nine years old. You see, Vera Marie, who was two and a half years old, had her urinary bladder removed, and it was obvious that unless something miraculous happened, she would die. My mother, who was Italian and a strong believer, decided to go to Italy in 1968 to see Padre Pio and ask him for a miracle. She took with her my oldest brother, Michael, who at the age of 11 was a strong boy; Christina, who was only one month old; and Vera, of course. Francesca, who was seven years old; Maria, who was five; and I stayed behind here in Pennsylvania with our father. My mother promised God that if Padre Pio would heal her daughter, she would dedicate her life to him. She went to his friary where she saw him; Padre Pio blessed her children, and Mom kissed his hand. When they got back home, Vera Marie was taken to the doctors, and they confirmed that a bladder had grown back. It was a miracle! My mother started prayer groups and giving lectures all through the world about Padre Pio and her experience with him. She later became one of the founders of this Centre for Padre Pio along with my father."

I am moved and thank her for sharing her beautiful story.

"Now let's return to you. Tell me three things that make you happy."

"Serving God by serving His people. If I say that I love God, how can I show it to Him? By serving His people in my humble capacity. I trust He will reward me a hundredfold, as He is never outdone in generosity.

"Another thing that makes me happy is knowing Padre Pio and how he has increased our faith and love. Although I never met him personally, through my mother and Padre Pio's teachings and attitude Padre Pio has kept this family together in peace. He has also taught us to trust completely in God.

"My other perhaps more selfish joy is my 16-and-a-half-year-old son. When my siblings were having children, I thought I would not be able to be so blessed, and I prayed and prayed to Our Lady and to Padre Pio. I used to talk to Padre Pio and argue with him and say, 'Padre Pio, I know you hear my prayers. Please don't let it take so long.' We tried to conceive a baby for five years. I promised Padre Pio that if he would give me a child, I would call him Santino Pio or her Santina Pia, like little Saint Pio. Padre Pio gave me my miracle: After almost six years of trying to conceive, I finally was with child and gave birth to a healthy little boy that we indeed named Santino Pio."

I feel tears welling up in my eyes.

"Julia, tell me some of the happiest moments in your life."

"Santino's birth was definitely one of the happiest moments in my life. There was also one day in my childhood that I think back on with a lot of happiness. It's a very personal memory of a very normal and simple day in my life when I was a little girl. It was an ordinary day, and my mother and I spent the whole day together doing nothing special: We cooked together, cleaned the house, did the laundry, and ate together. From morning to evening, we were together chatting, laughing, and appreciating doing little things for our family. I learned more that day than I ever realized. At the time I was five or six years old but I just clung to that day, and this memory saw me through my life. This day happened before Padre Pio came into our lives. I would always remember this day, and when my mother became very involved with Padre Pio and became the editor of the *Voice of Padre Pio* international magazine, the translator of books about his life, a lecturer who travelled extensively, and the founder of this Centre, I would think back and relive this day that we spent together and remind myself that despite of all the public light she was getting, my mother was first and foremost my mother."

"Julia, what do you do when you are feeling down in order to get happy again?"

"I pray my Rosary. I turn to Our Lady. Padre Pio taught us that the rosary is our weapon in all circumstances, and in this I find great comfort and immense joy."

Look at the positives of a negative
Sunday, 13 June

"My secret to happiness is just having a positive attitude. I simply don't see the point of sulking and being angry. It's not good for you nor for the people around you. You have to try to forget about things and move on. Even when you are faced with a situation that is not so good, try to look at it and act with a positive attitude: It will bring you and other people happiness, and a situation that originally seemed to be negative might actually turn into a great happy moment."

Isidora, 16 years old

Open yourself up to others
Monday, 14 June

"Excuse me, have you ever mailed a letter to Asia before?"

I turn to a beautiful Asian lady standing next to me in line at the post office.

"Yes, I mail letters to Japan all the time," she replies.

"I am mailing my first letter to my husband in Japan. Is it true that it takes a month?"

"No," she smiles, "it takes approximately a week."

Her name is Kyoko, and she tells me that she has finished a documentary that looks at the reasons why Japanese women leave Japan to come to New York. We speak for a long time and agree to meet again after her return from a film festival where her documentary will be shown.

Three weeks later we get together for lunch. Kyoko narrates her experience at the film festival. After a while she says, "It's your turn to ask me questions now, Elisabeth."

"One could say that when you left Japan to come here to work, it was also partly to follow your dream and to seek your own happiness, wasn't it?"

"Well, in order to fully understand the reason for my move, we have to go back in time. During high school I spent one year in the U.S. as an exchange student. After that I returned to Japan to finish my education where I was totally overworked. When I was 27 years old, I got a Fulbright scholarship to attend a journalist program at a university in the U.S. Suddenly, being a student again, my body started screaming, and I had to remove one ovary. I began thinking about life, my goals, and realized that I really wanted to have a child before another ovary got damaged. My husband joined me at the university for eight months, and I became pregnant.

"When my baby was 26 days old, I returned to Japan. I stayed at home with my daughter for four months and, after finding a nice nursery for her, I started working as a reporter for a network TV station again. I was among the first female reporters to have a baby and a job at the same time. I loved my job, was an aggressive reporter, spent less and less time with my baby, and felt constantly torn between the job and the guilt for not spending enough time with my child.

"When she was four or five years old, a media company in New York offered me a job in which I would cover the stock market. This will be perfect, I thought, because the stock exchange closes at 4 p.m. so I would have more time with my daughter and would get a better balance between work and family.

"And this is where we get to my quest for happiness: I thought I would find happiness when I came to this country in the spring of 2001. We got settled in a nice apartment one block away from the World Trade Center but in September of that same year we had to be evacuated. However, the help and the kindness we got from neighbors and friends were tremendous.

"It was after these struggles that I realized that happiness is always there; you don't have to travel to find it, you just have to identify it around you and let it find you by opening yourself up to others. You create your own happiness. After 9/11 I understood that it's ok to reach out for people, it's ok to ask for help. Maybe if I would have done that in Japan I would have been happier. In Japan I was too stressed to maintain friendships: It was all about my job and my daughter."

I look at her as she speaks. She is beautiful with big brown eyes, long black hair, and an elegant grey suit. Two delicate gold chains adorn her neck.

"Kyoko, tell me about some of the happiest moments in your life."

"In this high-tech world you can now make a movie in your own living room. Before I got a professional editor I used to do it myself. My daughter never thought I would be able to do this documentary. She is now 17 years old and had never been very comfortable having two cultures in one body. But after seeing the movie she became very proud of her double heritage and now embraces both her cultures. In her high school she has even started a tea-club, of which she is the vice-president; they get together and try teas from all over the world. One day my mom flew in from Japan and prepared a real Japanese tea ceremony for her tea-club. The fact that my movie changed her outlook on herself and who she is was a very poignant and happy moment in my life.

"I am sorry to be speaking so much about my movie but it is very important in my life right now. My movie had already been shown at a film festival in Tokyo. But when I was told that Miami and Tunis had also picked my screener out of the many others they get for their film festival, this made me extremely happy because I realized that my movie could be universal."

"What about happy moments in your career?"

"A happy moment in my career had to do with some friends I made when I was covering the earthquake in Kobe in 1995 and its aftermath for five years. After the earthquake took place, a large fire erupted. I went to the burned area and was introduced to a butcher family who had a girl who was in first grade. She and I immediately connected. She was such a sweet girl: She collected garbage from other stores but her smile and attitude and the way she cared for the elderly—many of whom had been severely burned from the fires—was very touching; the elderly loved her deeply and treated her very nicely. We kept in touch over the years so when they heard the news about September 11, they called me to see how I was doing. When I spoke with them, they told me that their daughter had majored in how to take care of elderly people. It made me very happy to see that she had found so much good out of a disaster."

My grandfather

Tuesday, 15 June

Sheila, one of my colleagues, is today's "happiness date."

"Tell me three things that make you happy."

"Sharing good food and wine with friends or going for a walk with a friend." She gives me a big, wicked smile. "Jewelry! Gold. It's like the cherry on the cake. A nice earring, a ring: You look at them all the time and say, 'This is truly nice!' It takes on a special value if you have received if from somebody you love who is deceased.

"The third thing that would make me happy is to be in love. I have never been in love. I have been 'in like.' Love is like a dirty diaper or a rose. It is a strange thing but I would like to know what it is about."

"Are you looking for somebody?"

"I am open. I'm from the old school; I want a man who can do stuff with his hands, who is not afraid of getting dirty, who doesn't dress nicer than a woman, and who opens the door for me, even though I say 'no.' I want a man who cuts the lawn, even if he has enough money to pay somebody to do it for him.

"My grandfather was my first love. One of my nicest memories was the time I spent with him as a child, between the age of six to 14 years old. He lived in South Carolina, and every summer vacation I would go and visit him. He used to call me 'boy,' and we used to box. When he came back from work at the Navy yard, I would wait for him on the porch, and he would always have a sweet for me. He taught me how to draw. His colleagues and people from church would say that he was a 'man's man.' I think that already as a child you have set up a definition for what kind of man you want."

"What are your tricks to get happy again when you are down or angry?"

"Leave me alone! When I am down, I recoil. You can tell by my face, my clothes, and by the way I walk. Usually people will shy away from me. I like to be short and intense about it though: Prolonged sadness takes too much energy. I also believe that sadness makes you stronger and that happiness makes you weaker."

"Why do you say that happiness makes you weaker?"

"If you are always happy, you don't improve. If everything is fine, you want to stay in your happy little bubble. But when you are sad, you look within yourself. When people feel sad, they tend to be honest about their shortcomings and with themselves about who they are. You come out stronger because of that."

"Sheila, one last question: Are you happy?"

"No but I am learning how to be happy. You have to learn about what makes you happy, and you have to work for your happiness. I want to experience love. Although I am not happy, I am learning to be at peace with myself, although there is a missing piece: love."

The day I came out of jail
Saturday, 19 June

Michael is washing off the last traces of paint from his hands. He has come for a few hours to finish a painting job at our home. He is approximately six feet, five inches, with blue eyes and a great sense of humor.

"What is happiness?" I ask him.

He seems in deep thought. "I have never had to describe it before," he answers with a heavy Brooklyn accent. "The happiness thing is my wife. I call her my wife but we never married. I don't see the point in that. She is my life partner. There is no need to fix something if it is not broken. Also loving my family and friends, and being loved back. Getting respect. I love funny people. My kids: That's my definition of happiness. Waking up and seeing my kids smile giving me a hug. Every time I see my kids my heart explodes."

"What were some of the happiest moments in your life?"

"The birth of my two children, the day I met my wife, and the day I came out of prison in April 1996. In my youth I hung out with the wrong crowd, partied a lot, smoked marijuana, and had a lot of women. One day the police caught me for possession of drugs and an illegal firearm—I used to keep it in the dashboard of my car—and I was sent to jail for 16 and a half months."

I am looking at the tattoos on his arms while he mentions jail. He pulls up his sleeve and shows me the picture of a skull smoking a cigarette, wearing a hat, and pulling a gun.

"This depicted me in jail. I was dead, I didn't have a life. That's the skull. I had a gangster hat; I used to smoke and carry a gun. I also have one down here in the lower pelvic region that says, 'All you can eat.'" He giggles.

"How was jail?"

"It changed my life. I thought and thought. It made me a better man and gave me sobriety. One month after I got out of jail I met my wife. She asked me, 'What do you want to do with your life?' I told her I wanted a woman in my life, children, and a home. That was it. We started the journey together. For me, life is simple."

"How would you end this sentence: 'In order to be happy, you have to...'?"

"In order to be happy, you have to live life to the fullest and don't do anything you will regret tomorrow. You only have one life so live it!"

"Michael, are you happy?"

"Yeah, I have a beautiful family. I wake up every day, and although I do not believe in God, I must say that I have Heaven in my hat!"

As he pulls out of the driveway, he lowers the window.

"Why don't you also throw in there somewhere: Smile! Don't be afraid to help! Be nice! Be generous with people."

Playing the piano
Monday, 21 June

"One thing that brings me great joy is playing on the piano or the organ but also when I can make other people happy through my music. A particularly moving experience was when I played *On the Wings of Song* of Mendelssohn for my grandfather. He was very sick, and it was the day before he was going to the hospital. He was sitting in his blue chair in the living room, and I was playing at the grand piano. My grandfather cried when I played it. This was the last time I played for him, and he never returned home from the hospital."

Haakon, cousin in Norway

Happiness in the eyes of a five-year-old
Wednesday, 23 June

When my colleague Marie brings her five-year-old son Ryan to the office, I see a wonderful opportunity for a nice interview. After I give his plump cheeks some gentle kisses, he climbs up on the chair and looks at me intently while dangling his feet and giving me a big smile.

"Tell me some things that make you happy."

"Kindness, when people are being nice, not fighting, but helping each other."

"Who is the nicest person in the whole world?"

"My mother, actually, my whole family."

"I have heard that you are very helpful at home."

"I always do the dishes. My mom puts the soap in, and I am the one who gets to wash them." He smiles proudly.

"Name another thing that makes you happy."

"Friends. I have a lot of friends. In my class there are 20 kids. We have fun together, and the best part is that they are all nice to each other."

"I have a very difficult question for you, okay?" I put on a serious face.

He nods and seems very curious as to what I am about to ask him.

"What is happiness to you?"

"That's not a difficult question. Happiness is when you..." he stops, leans his chin against the palm of his hand, and after a while exclaims, "Got it! Happiness is when you do exactly what the teacher wants you to do, and you get wonderful things from the teacher."

"You have a nice teacher. What does the teacher give you?"

"When we behave we get special surprises. She usually gives us ice cream, and when you go home she gives us gifts. One day she gave me a helicopter."

"What's your favorite ice cream flavor?"

"All of them."

Ryan starts to get a little bit restless and keeps moving his feet but does his best to remain focused.

"What were some of the happiest moments in your life?"

"I will think about that." He remains silent. "That's the most difficult question."

I let him ponder about it for a while.

"The first time when I was very happy was the day I was born."

"Do you remember that?"

"Yes, I remember because I have seen pictures."

"What were other moments when you were very happy?"

"When I go to school and learn. One time I was so happy because I went to visit my dad, and we went to the swimming pool together with my brother."

"I love all your answers. Now try to finish this sentence: 'For somebody to be happy, they have to…'"

He hesitates for a short while. "For somebody to be happy, they have to spend most of their time loving their children."

Excavations from past cultures
Sunday, 27 June

It is dusk when we start climbing the steep, winding cobblestone streets in the old city of Toledo. They are narrow and sparsely lit with old lampposts, creating a magical atmosphere. Voices and laughter resonate from restaurants and bars nearby.

We have just finished dinner and are struggling to find our way back to the car. But even with a map, which is hard to read due to insufficient light, it feels as if we are in a labyrinth. Suddenly, as we are standing at an intersection of four streets with not a soul in view, a man with beige slacks and an open linen short-sleeve shirt comes strolling down the street. He has a mustache and white hair, and a faint smell of wine and a hint of sweat emanate from him. I guess he has just returned from a nice meal and a few drinks with friends. This is the second time we have bumped into him this evening. Earlier on when he heard us speak English, he had wished us a good evening and asked us where we were from.

"Excuse me, sir, but we are trying to go back to our car. Where are we on this map?"

"You are here. If you go up that way, you will come to the old Jewish part of town, and if you go down that way, you get to the Moorish part of town."

I realize that I have not yet interviewed anybody today so I ask him if he will agree to an interview.

"As long as it is short," he replies.

"What makes you happy?"

"My discoveries. I am a Catholic but of Jewish ancestry. I am an electrical mine engineer and used to work in the mines in the United Arab Emirates, France, and in South Africa. I am a '*Toledano*' (somebody from Toledo), and when I retired I decided to buy a house in the old Jewish quarters of the city. Toledo is the city of three cultures—Arab, Jewish, and Christian—but the Visigoths and the Romans were here, too. Archeologically, it's a very rich city. When I bought my house I started doing excavations in my own home, and under it I discovered a Jewish settlement. The Jews came to Toledo in the seventh century."

"Are you still excavating?"

"Yes, the work is still going on. I am sure you have noticed how winding the streets are here?"

I nod.

"Well, it's because they were built to fit in between the houses, whose walls are approximately 70 cm in width. My house is right up the street here. Would you like to see it?"

"Oh yes!"

We follow him for a couple of hundred feet until we arrive at a street corner where a sign reads: "The Jewish Neighborhood."

"Have you ever shown your discoveries to anybody?"

"Yes, but only to Palestinians, Jews, and Arabs. Not to Christians because they did the Inquisition and destroyed so much of other people's culture."

I thank him, and he enters his house. My son, his friend, and I finally find our way out of the maze of the old city and return to our car.

You are a gardener of happiness
Monday, 28 June

Salamanca! The most famous university town in Spain. While the boys are relaxing in the hotel after a long drive, I head toward the nearby park in search of a "happiness date." I sit down on a bench. After a few minutes a man appears at the end of the street, walking in my direction. I am excited at the thought of having found someone. Suddenly, he stops, opens up his zipper, and starts urinating behind a lamppost. I change my mind and quickly return to the hotel.

The entrance hall is empty; only the receptionist is there. She smiles as soon as she sees me. From her name tag I learn that her name is Ines. She appears to be in her late 40s, has short black hair, black-rimmed glasses, and wears a navy-blue dress jacket and skirt.

"Tell me three things that make you happy."

"To see the sun. Light always gives me happiness.

"To see another person smile or laugh. This means that they are happy.

"To watch children. The simple innocence of children breeds happiness. Where there is a young child, there are no adults in a bad mood because they make you laugh. The sad thing is that we lose this when we become adults."

Her voice is kind and gentle, her words simple and yet so beautiful.

"You are a gardener of happiness because you are planting seeds for happiness, and all those who plant seeds will always reap happiness."

July

Drink, eat, and be merry!

Thursday, 1 July

Leaving behind the picturesque city of Santiago de Compostela with its magnificent cathedral and devout pilgrims, we continue our drive down the coast of Galicia until we reach Cambados, a small fishing village.

It is nearing eight o'clock. Only four more hours to find a "happiness date!" The boys are thrilled when I tell them they can stay in the hotel and order room service while I go for a stroll amid white-washed cobblestone streets and small plazas where people are gathering.

A couple laughing loudly at a table nearby draws my attention. I go closer. There is something familiar about them.

"Excuse me, haven't I seen you before?"

Then it hits me. They had been eating next to us the previous night in Santiago de Compostela. They invite me for a drink and suggest I join them for supper. I gladly accept. David has a nice tan, short, slightly ruffled hair, an eagle nose, and the smile of a cheeky young boy. He seems older than Michelle, who has long reddish hair, blue eyes, and freckles. She is very pretty. They both puff leisurely at their cigarettes while drinking and eating. The evening goes by quickly. Laughter fills the air.

As the main course is nearing an end, I ask if I can interview one of them.

"David, why don't you go ahead? I would actually like to know what you think about happiness," Michelle says.

David's tanned cheeks have now taken on a slightly pink color; as a matter of fact I think we all look pretty healthy at that point of the evening!

"Ok, if you want," he says good-heartedly. "I like the sun because you just feel warm and happy. My favorite occupation would be eating in the sun while listening to music. Eating is a second thing that makes me happy.

"New experiences and lovely places: I am very much into lovely places. Oh! And motorbikes! I have a Kawasaki 600. My favorite thing in life would be to tour around Italy on my motorbike."

He takes a sip of wine and a drag of his cigarette.

"It's really sad, isn't it?" he says with his British accent, "I am a rather shallow person: I just like enjoying myself! No responsibilities! It's pathetic but true!"

We laugh.

"What is happiness?"

"Happiness is everything that is not being uptight, depressed, or chained to a job or children. It's being free, independent, rich, no ties, and able to enjoy yourself!"

"What were some of the happiest moments in your life?"

"Touring around Europe on my motorbike. Every year I used to go for six to eight weeks without knowing where I was going and staying in youth hostels. That was just smashing! When I look back at my life, lying on the beaches in India stand out as very happy moments. I like having a few drinks and spending a good time with friends. I also love to watch people."

He pauses and becomes pensive. "My problem in life is that I don't have enough interests. I don't have major euphoric moments unless I use ecstasy. But then I don't get depressed either."

Michelle interrupts, "Yes, you do have euphoric moments!"

He looks at her quizzically.

"The breakfast this morning at the parador of Santiago where they served caviar, smoked salmon, sour cream, and melba toast!"

"You are so right, darling! You see, food once more! I would love to have a yacht, go to different ports, and just drop off at nice restaurants. What I do enjoy, by the way, is opera and ballet!"

"Are you happy, David?"

He looks at Michelle.

"Don't look at me, David!" she replies laughingly. "You have to say what you think."

"Well, you have known me for 20 years. Oh well, then, I think I am happy."

Michelle adds, "All our friends think he has the nicest life. They would like to have his philosophy of life: Avoid hard work at all cost. When I first met David he told me, 'True freedom is the ability to earn money so you don't have to work.' He later developed more wonderful quotes such as 'Try to get the maximum return from the minimum effort.'"

Have a sense of wonderment
Sunday, 4 July

Exploring the majestic medieval walls of Avila with its many turrets will easily make you forget about conducting interviews. The sun had been strong, temperatures high, and the kids are tired. We return to the hotel so they can relax for a while. Resting for them means interview time for me.

Down in the hotel bar a man is sitting by himself, having a beer and reading the newspaper. His name is Chris; he is British and has lived in Avila for the past 16 years with his Spanish wife. He must be in his late 40s with a blondish beard and blue eyes.

"Chris, tell me three things that make you happy."

"Being with my two sons, James and Oliver. We have travelled quite a lot together. This summer my oldest son will spend two weeks in a soccer camp away from home, and I realize that pretty soon we won't be able to spend holidays together anymore. It makes me sad to think about that.

"Indian food makes me happy. I cook it, and when I am not in Spain, I seek it out whether it is London, New York, the Far East, or South East Asia.

"Music really gives me pleasure. It's one of the few things that puts a smile on my face, even when England is out of the World Cup. My first musical memory goes back to 1976-77 when punk music happened. I got to see some fabulous bands, and it inspired me to take up the guitar. A few years ago a friend of mine and I started a duet, and two weeks ago he and I did a concert in a pub here in Avila to raise money for the fight against cancer. We raised 1,000 Euros in one night.

"I would like to add a fourth thing. Encourage people to develop their talents so they don't have to look back with any regrets. And lastly, the smell of a bookshop, the papers and the books, makes me really happy."

He orders another beer for himself and one for me, too. You get thirsty conducting interviews!

"What were some of the happiest moments in your life, Chris?"

"The summer of 1976. It was at that time when summer holidays seemed to go on forever. It was the hottest summer in England. I had my first girlfriend, and there was a new musical soundtrack as a backdrop to enjoy all this. That summer was also a very happy summer for my parents, which made me very happy, too."

His voice is melodious and lively, and I feel carried away with his memories.

"The first time I went to New York was in 1990. I was writing lyrics for this band with whom I travelled and was blown away by all the different people and the skyscrapers in New York. We recorded at the Chrysler building and had two concerts in Long Island in a comedy club where Eddie Murphy had started his career. It was also during the Summer Olympics final. The U.S. had not quite understood soccer so they cut when there was a penalty shot."

"What is your definition of happiness, Chris?"

"Happiness is not having any kind of hatred in your heart. Hatred will just wear you down on the inside. If you can make a conscious effort to accept that there will always be differences, then you will feel happier yourself, and hatred will disappear.

"Happiness is also having a sense of wonderment about everything around us and realizing how lucky we are to be here!"

"Are you happy?"

"A resounding yes!"

Don't force a flower to grow
Tuesday, 6 July

Hasta la vista, España! New York, here we come! We are on the plane heading back home. As I get up to stretch my legs, I meet Leonardo, a flight attendant from Guatemala, who shares his views on happiness with me.

"I am going to tell you something really silly but in order to be happy, we are supposed to just be and breathe. It's really very simple. You are not supposed to stress yourself. You don't force a flower to grow. God created the universe a certain way. Don't get sucked up into problems because they will always exist. Sometimes life is difficult to understand but that's ok. We don't have to understand."

Without sadness, no happiness
Sunday, 11 July

"In order to be happy, you have to feel sadness or any other emotions that are not happy. If you are always happy, you wouldn't know why it is so good, and there would be nothing special about happiness. Part of happiness is being sad."

Nissim, 16 years old

Miracles
Monday, 12 July

Martha, my cousin's wife, and I are having lunch. She is in her mid-50s, marvels at small pleasures in life, and has tons of energy. She has blond hair cut in a bob and brown-framed glasses. I ask her to name a few happy moments in her life.

"I have seen Jesus do a lot of miracles," she replies. "In my younger years, while taking my Master's degree, I used to work as a registrar in an emergency room. One day a man was rushed in; his throat had swollen, and he had not breathed for a long time. I had to call the family to tell them to get to the hospital as quickly as possible. I spoke with the father of the patient, who was a Christian, and found out that the patient was a 36-year-old male, married with two children. Together with some colleagues from the hospital, we all prayed over the phone. The patient later woke up and was totally well. The doctors said it was a miracle and that he should have been brain dead. After the man woke up, I went to speak to him and told him we had prayed for him, and that God must have had a very special plan for him to give him back his life.

"I also witnessed another miracle in the emergency room. As I was checking in the patients, I could hear a lady howling in the room next to the emergency room. I went to see her. She informed me that her 17-year-old son had just been diagnosed with an aneurism of the brain, and the recent EEG they had taken showed that he was brain dead. They were just waiting for the heart to stop. She told me that a few years before she had lost her daughter. We prayed and prayed but seemingly to no avail. As they were putting his body on the gurney, his body started flopping like a fish, then he sat up and asked, 'Where am I?'"

I let it all sink in.

"Can I tell you one more story?" She laughs. "I like to tell ghost stories, especially holy ghost stories."

I nod excitedly.

"One afternoon I was sitting near an escalator at a shopping mall in Norway with Flavius, a French student who lived with us for six months. As I was helping him with some Norwegian vocabulary, our eyes wandered to the escalator. We saw a man lying flat on his back. He had had a heart attack. Paramedics came, and for 25 minutes they tried to shock him with electrical shocks.

"'Let's pray, Flavius!' I said. I prayed and prayed and prayed, and even spoke in tongues. I did not care what other people would think about me. I prayed that God would heal him and raise him from the dead. When they returned to put him on the gurney, he was breathing.

"To me, one of the things that make me the happiest in the world is to tune in to the power of the Lord and serve Him by making other people happy."

It could be you

Tuesday, 13 July

A beautiful black lady sits down next to me on the train. Her name is Sherly, and she is from Honduras. She is very enthusiastic about my project.

"Tell me three things that make you happy."

"My family, my friends, and my job. I am a social worker for a hospital with mentally ill people. It is a community-based program through which patients do not have to be in institutions but can be at home, in group homes, or with family. Ever since I was a child I wanted to help others. Every day I visit patients. We escort them to the doctor and make sure they take their medication. For some of them, we are their only friends."

"What is the best part of your job?"

"I like the twists of the mind, the switch, the unexpected, the unpredictability of the people. People can be very sick today, get hospitalized for three or four months, and then get much better. It can happen as a result of a shock, an unexpected event. We need to have compassion. It teaches you not to be judgmental and to be a better person. Don't look at how they dress or how they speak. Look at the inside. It could be you."

She pauses. "The third thing that makes me happy is my accomplishments. I came to this country when I was 18 years old, didn't know the language, and had to get adjusted to the culture. I did earn an associate degree in liberal arts, then a Master's in Education and Social Work. By achieving my degrees I feel confident that I can accomplish anything I set my heart to. I want to give credit to my husband, though, who has stayed with our four kids all these years. He used to be an aviation mechanic back home but put his career on hold to raise our children. I could not have done what I did without him. In a couple of years I will take care of the kids, and he will go back to school and further his education."

I am grateful to be in the United States

Wednesday, 21 July

The late afternoon sun is creating a warm glow on the lake. Two people are rowing leisurely in a small boat. A young Hispanic lady sits on one of the benches facing the lake while watching two young children play. Her name is Alma; she came to the U.S. four years ago.

"Tell me three things that make you happy."

"My children. I have this little *gordita* (chubby one) Mariana, who has just turned one, and a son, Jose Ismail, who is three years old. He is in Mexico with my mother. My mother and my husband also make me very happy. My father is dead.

"I am also very grateful to be in the United States and for my work at Barnes & Noble where I price books. When I go out to dance *duranguense*, which is a genre of Mexican music—it doesn't happen too often but when it does—I really enjoy myself."

Alma is holding Mariana against her chest who, with her little fingers, is pulling at her shirt. She starts feeding her. Mariana is wearing a white-layered dress with pink and blue flowers and sandals decorated with flowers. She has big, brown eyes, a nice tanned complexion, and smiles easily.

"How would you end this sentence: 'In order to be happy, you have to…'?"

"In order to be happy, you have to live life fully every day and be cheerful because you never know what tomorrow will bring."

Impossible happiness
Friday, 23 July

At the bookstore I meet a young woman with black hair pulled back in a ponytail, her brown eyes further accentuated by a dark kohl stick.

"Tell me three things that make you happy."

"When there is peace in my family, and we all get along. I also like listening to music, learning about art, painting, and drawing. When I was younger I used to play the saxophone, and I still play the piano." She reflects for a while. "When I find something I am talented at, when I overcome an obstacle, and succeed in something hard such as school, and I feel that I can actually go somewhere with my life."

"What is your dream?"

"In September I will be a sophomore at the university where I take Visual Arts. My big dream is to go to UCLA in California, start my own graphic design company, and move to Los Angeles. But I don't think my parents will allow me to live away from the house because they don't want me to live in a dorm. You see, my sister once lived in a dorm, and they got so mad at her. They wanted her to remain a virgin until the day she got married. My father, who is from the Middle East, disowned her and did not speak to her for six months. After that, they won't allow me to sleep over at her place or to spend too much time with her. They are very strict with me."

"That must be really hard. How would you define 'happiness'?"

"It's a state of mind without suffering, where your soul doesn't feel like it's ripping apart. Happiness is impossible because you can never reach full contentment."

"Why should happiness be impossible?"

She is silent for a moment. "I can never be fully happy because I am living a lie. You see, I am a lesbian and have to hide this from my parents. My father would certainly disown me if he found out."

"I just returned from a gay wedding in Spain," I add, wanting her to feel better.

She looks at me nostalgically.

"Tell me about some of the happiest moments in your life."

A flicker of a smile crosses her face as she continues. "A few months ago I went to see my best friends in Arizona, whom I had not seen for six years. This vacation was one of the happiest moments in my life because I went without my parents. It's sad to say but sometimes happiness is not being with them." She looks down. "Another happy day was when I snuck out of my house last summer. My mom and I had been arguing, and she was not going to allow me to go out. I decided to elope. I had placed a comforter on the floor so it wouldn't creek when I tread on it. I had already opened the lock of the front door—it usually makes a lot of noise when turned—I had programmed the television to stop at 12:30 p.m., and I snuck out to meet my girlfriend, who was waiting for me in her car outside. I was very happy that day because it was scary and exciting at the same time." She pauses. "Can I tell you another happy moment in my life? It was June 28, and I was watching the Gay Pride Parade. It was the day before my girlfriend asked me out. I remember feeling in a safe haven and that I didn't have to hide myself."

Appreciate what you have
Saturday, 24 July

"In order to be happy, you have to appreciate what you have. One of the worst traits human beings have is that we quickly become content with our lot and then we want more. I remember my mother telling me a story about my father. He was born in Moscow and immigrated to the U.S. For the first four years he was on welfare, and life was very hard for him and my mother. She recalled seeing all the different goods in the shelves at the supermarket, and she could only dream about buying them. They used food stamps and had to be extremely careful how they spent them. Then my father started his own business, and when it really took off she vividly remembers that she could go to the supermarket and buy whatever she wanted: She was elated. Three months later this feeling was gone. You have to be grateful and make happiness last."

Brian, New York investor

Performing my job the right way
Tuesday, 27 July

An older man who looks like Jack Lemmon with white hair, wearing beige khaki pants, running shoes, white undershirt, and gold chains around his neck, is sitting by himself in the train. His name is Jesus; he is originally from the Dominican Republic and has kind, lively eyes.

"Tell me three things that make you happy."

"Seeing you smile, performing my work the right way—I am a mechanical engineer and I work for the Metro North Railroad, and seeing my two Maltese puppies, Peppy and Snowy, doing well."

"What is your definition of happiness?"

"For me, happiness is having what you need when you need it, being healthy, seeing people do the right thing, children laughing, and vacations."

"Are you happy, Jesus?"

"Yes, I am happy but I could be happier."

"What would make you happier?"

"I would be happier if I had more money; not for me but for my family in the Dominican Republic. We are nine brothers and sisters, and I have three children. Some family members are poor, and if I had more money I would make sure they all went to university, became independent, and did not do bad things."

Choose happiness

Wednesday, 28 July

"In order to be happy, you have to deliberately and consciously look on the bright side. I have grieved for people, lost people, gone through challenging times, but I cannot say that I wasn't happy. My husband and I had a very hard time conceiving our twins. We tried for a long while but I couldn't get pregnant so we had to get help. These were trying times, often with false good news. We would get disappointed and sad. However, as much as I have not forgotten these times, I chose to be happy, to focus on the good things instead of the bad ones. I think happiness is a conscious choice."

Amber, NJ Transit

Serve people in need
Saturday, 31 July

An Indian gentleman with black glasses in a heavy square frame, sunglasses attached to his shirt, and short, black hair sits alone at a table at the café.

"Excuse me, sir, may I ask you a question?"

He looks up.

"I won't ask for your last name nor do I need to use your first name. I don't have a blog. I just write this for myself."

After having been turned down earlier for an interview, I thought it would be good to reassure my next prospect. He smiles and invites me to sit. His name is Shree.

"Tell me some things that make you happy."

"When I have a very good conversation with somebody, and it is spontaneous, not pre-planned and with no ulterior motives. Look at your project, for instance. You felt that you had to reassure me, that you weren't going to ask for the last name, etc. In this country—I have been in this country for 11 years now—people are always thinking, second-guessing 'what's behind this and that?' A person approaches you, and you always think 'what does he or she want?' Your thought is very simple yet you still have to explain it to people. In India they would love to talk to you.

"When I serve somebody who is in real need, that makes my day. On Friday, for instance, when the conductor had passed, somebody stood up and said he was going to Long Island but he didn't have enough money for his train ticket. I didn't know whether he was lying or not. I didn't care. Didn't want to think about that. Let's assume he was lying. What was I going to lose? Five bucks? What if it was real? As soon as I started to give, other passengers followed. If it served its purpose, it was a nice feeling. We should take an initiative to come forward to help. I might be fooled many times but I haven't changed according to the circumstances. If you change your notion about people, you lose yourself."

"What is your definition of happiness?"

"Happiness is when you make yourself available to serve people in need. You can invite people for dinner. That's nice but they have food. Do we invite people for dinner who don't' have food? It doesn't have to be a country; if one person starts giving, it will become a trickle effect."

August

Make it happen
Sunday, 1 August

"In order to be happy, you have to make happen the things you want to come true for yourself. You cannot do everything you want in life. Ninety years might seem like a long time but time passes by very quickly."

Karl, customer at the mall

You decide what makes you happy
Wednesday, 4 August

My colleague Hatem, who is from Yemen, and I are having lunch. When asked to name what makes him happy, he smiles.

"I think it is me. If my happiness depends on something or somebody, I cannot be happy. If *I* decide that a certain thing will make me happy or not happy, it is what I decide that makes me happy, not the thing itself. There are not only three things that make me happy but as many as I want to, as I decide there should be. It's all up to my mind.

"If I feel down in the morning, I take a white piece of paper, a pen, and write in big letters: 'I will be happy' (or any other feeling that I may want to achieve during the day). Then I stick it on the wall. I will look at it on my way to the bathroom, when I have my coffee, when I grab my coat to leave the house. By the time I reach the office I try to hold on to this feeling. It is, of course, very difficult to control your emotions, though.

"Emotions are what you believe they are. There is nothing called sadness or discomfort, which is still very normal for a human being, unless you make it."

Make others happy

Monday, 9 August

As I am walking down the cars of the train in search of a "happiness date," I notice a young man with brown hair, a cap, blue t-shirt, and jeans stained by white paint. He is looking out of the window. The seat next to him is empty. When I tell him about my happiness project, he is excited and eager to be interviewed. His name is Connor, 17 years old.

"Name a few things that make you happy."

"When I see people that I love accomplish something, for instance, when my older brother, after graduating from college, was chosen to be part of the Minor League in baseball, and when I am able to make other people happy. Last week I went for a one-week sleepover camp for kids who have cancer. There were about 70 children, and all came from a hospital. Quite a few had sickle cell anemia, others leukemia. Every day we did a lot of activities."

"Connor, what were some of the happiest moments in your life?"

"As a kid, I used to play baseball. I particularly remember being with my friends on the field, my parents watching and cheering for me. I loved to play under the lights. At that time there was nothing else to worry about.

"Every summer for many years my parents, three brothers, and some friends of ours would go camping for one week in Albany. We used to go to a cliff, which stood 50 feet over the lake, and although I was the youngest, I would always be the first one to jump off that cliff into the water.

"I am very happy when I go to high school dances. I love to dance, and when I get on the dance floor, I feel like I am lightening up the crowd."

"How would you end this sentence: 'In order to be happy, you have to…'?"

"In order to be happy, you have to be comfortable with who you are. As long as you are, that's all that matters. You have to love yourself, and then it's hard to let anyone put you down."

Never give up on your dreams
Tuesday, 10 August

"In order to be happy, you have to listen to yourself and your dreams. Don't do things just because other people tell you to do so and think you should. Everything is possible; no dream is too big if you just apply yourself. Try to be open-minded and surround yourself with positive people."

Jessica, lady at Barnes & Noble

An unexpected kiss
Thursday, 12 August

An African American gentleman with a small mustache and dreadlocks is reading a comic book at one of the tables in the bookstore.

"Excuse me, would you mind answering a few questions about happiness?" I ask, interrupting him.

He seems intrigued by the idea and invites me to sit down with him. His name is Ramon. He was born in the Bronx but his family immigrated from Panama.

"Ramon, tell me three things that make you happy."

"Waking up," he quickly answers.

"Why do you say that?"

"Because not waking up would suck."

"I like that!" I laugh.

"Every day is a brand-new slate of opportunities, things to do, and new people to meet," he adds as his second item. "The third thing that makes me happy is simple pleasures."

"Can you name some simple pleasures that make you happy?"

"Speaking to someone new, a stranger, and getting an unexpected hug or kiss before leaving. Going out dancing and getting a kiss. Getting a kiss that leaves the other person wanting more." His voice is smooth and melodious. His words are simple yet intimate, and I have the impression that he is tasting every word before uttering it. A closeness has been created between us. Everything else—the store, the people, the noise from the street—seem to have disappeared as he speaks; it is just him and me.

"Does this happen to you often?"

"Yes, quite often."

"Ramon, what is your definition of happiness?"

"Peace of mind."

"And what are some of the happiest moments in your life?"

He looks straight ahead, remembering. "My first kiss. I was 13 years old, behind a church in the Bronx. It was the girl who took the initiative. I was totally taken by surprise and shocked. I can still recall the chilling of my spine, the sweat between my fingers, and the feeling of breathing for the first time."

He thinks for a while before speaking again, then goes on slowly, remembering. "It was a random day in June. I had my dog with me. I was on the beach and had brought a lawn chair. I was playing with my dog. I threw the ball in the water. She threw herself in there, picked up the ball, came back wet, wiped herself, sat down next to me, and huffed. I looked down at her: She was looking out at the ocean. I started looking at the ocean, too. Then it hit me. 'This is cool. I even have two days left of my vacation.' It was a really nice day. I was sipping on—what was it again? Yeah, some lemonade and eating chocolate chip cookies. The dog was drinking water and eating chocolate chip cookies, too. That was a really great day!"

As he speaks, I can almost feel the wind in my hair, the sand under my feet, and smell of the wetness of the dog, the taste of chocolate cookies and lemonade. I am at the beach, watching the sea and the rolling of the waves. No, wait: We are at Barnes & Noble.

"Ramon, are you happy?"

"Oh yeah! Every day I have the opportunity to change the course of my life: I am very happy about that. In life, there are cycles: After the storm there will be calmness, after the rain the sun. That's why you have to seize the moment and go for it without breaking any vows or rules."

My lunch hour has ended. I take his hand and hope to convey my heartfelt thanks for his trust in me. I smile on my way back to the office. For a while I am still in a different world.

While typing up my notes in the train after work, one question keeps assailing me: Should I have given him a kiss?

Overcome old patterns

Monday, 16 August

I walk briskly up Madison Avenue, and as soon as I reach the Promenade at the Rockefeller Center, I notice him immediately. He seems so relaxed, enjoying every puff of his cigarette while studying the passersby on Fifth Avenue. His head is shaved, and he has a short, blond-greying beard.

"Excuse me, sir? May I ask you a question?"

"As long as you are not selling anything or trying to convert me into something I am not, you can sit down, and I will answer all the questions you want me to answer!" he replies laughingly. His name is Bernd, and he is visiting from Germany.

"Tell me three things that make you happy."

"When I realize that I treat my kids better than what my father did, and that I have overcome family patterns."

"Are you able to overcome family patterns?"

"This is my everyday challenge: 80% of the time I do, and 20% of the time I will do the old shit. Sometimes my son will pull these triggers that could create similar reactions that my father had but when I realize this, I try to change.

"Reflection and growing together makes me happy. Sometimes my wife and I will have an argument but if we both see what each of us did wrong, this will create a good and strong relationship. We have been together for almost eight years now and are growing together. Unless you develop this type of relationship, you will break up and never be able to grow old together: Both spouses have to learn about themselves and the other, and grow together."

He has finished his cigarette and looks intermittently at me or at the street when he needs to gather his thoughts.

"How would you end this sentence: 'In order to be happy, you have to…'?"

"In order to be happy, you have to overcome old patterns, learn who you really are and who you are not, and who you want to be in ten years from now, and put it into practice."

"Do you know who you are?"

"At some points I think I know who I am but then it changes. I discover something new. It never ends, it constantly flows, but that is growth. I am not so focused on happiness but I am more interested in self-discovery, self-experience, and in being astounded by all the small miracles in life around us. Each of us has an inner stillness, where you don't act nor react, and from this spot, from this inner silence, you can decide what direction to take and what to do. In order to find that spot, there is only one exercise: meditation. Every day for 20 minutes I sit and meditate, focusing only on my breath while I let the thoughts flow freely. I have done this for the last 15 to 20 years."

"What were some of the happiest moments in your life?"

"The birth of my children. Everything else are by-products."

"Are you happy, Bernd?"

"Yes, I am. I am a lucky man. One of the Zen masters that I have recorded once told me, 'It's not a miracle to walk on water but to walk on earth.' This is a once-in-a-lifetime opportunity that we have."

Holding hands with my husband
Saturday, 21 August

An older lady with white, short hair, blue eyes, a light blue t-shirt, and white trousers is reading a book by herself at one of the tables at Barnes & Noble.

"Excuse me!"

She looks up.

"May I ask you a question, please?"

She smiles and nods. Her name is Anita. I finish introducing my project when an elderly gentleman walks toward her.

"I am so sorry. I thought you were alone," I say apologetically.

"Oh, that's fine! I can tell you what makes me happy. My husband. I cannot imagine a more wonderful husband! I have nothing to complain about. He accepts me the way I am, and he is very tolerant of me, even if sometimes I might not exactly act as I am supposed to. We have been married for 58 years," she says dreamily.

By now Jim, her husband, has left to give us some privacy.

"How old were you when you married him?"

She thinks for a while. "I was old enough to know better."

"What else makes you happy?"

"My two daughters: Deirdra, who adopted twin boys—one is blond and the other one is a brunette—and Taryn, who lives in what I always call 'the frozen north' and has one daughter."

"How old are your daughters?"

"Let me see…hum…" She tries to remember. "I don't know." She looks around. "Where is Jim? He could have helped me. He has become my dictionary these days."

She doesn't seem too bothered by this lack of memory.

"Anita, what is your definition of happiness?"

"Happiness is having a good health. I don't wear glasses, and I enjoy reading. My husband, too. We come to Barnes & Noble frequently. Although Jim goes to Sloan Kettering, you know for that cancer that many men get, but he seems to be doing ok."

"Tell me some of the happiest moments in your life."

"When I was younger, I was a singer. I was a paid soloist in churches. I still have people stop me in church who say I have a beautiful voice. Other happy moments were having our daughters and raising them."

At regular intervals, she looks around for Jim. "Where is he?"

Jim returns. He is reading *Newsweek*.

"Anita, how would you end this sentence: 'In order to be happy, you have to…'?"

"In order to be happy, you have to have children who love you and who don't really mind taking care of you. Whenever we go somewhere, they come and pack our bags. My daughters are at my fingertips."

"Anita, are you happy?"

"Oh yes, very! I couldn't be happier! This man puts his hand in mine, and I love it!"

My job
Wednesday, 25 August

A lady with shoulder-length brown hair is reading a book while leaning against the window of the train. I tell her I am writing a book about happiness. She invites me to sit next to her. Her name is Olga. She is originally from St. Petersburg but has lived in the U.S. for 13 years.

"Tell me three things that make you happy."

"Going to the opera, theatre, and ballet, and spending time with my kids." She covers her mouth and blushes slightly. "I feel kind of embarrassed now. I probably should have started by mentioning our twin girls. They are brand new. They are fraternal twins and will be turning one year old on 7 September. They are a lot of fun, and now they are almost ready to walk, starting to cruise between furniture.

"Something else that makes me happy is something I don't do anymore: It's really my job. I used to teach and do research in German and Applied Linguistics as an Assistant Professor at university. This fall I will teach German at Rutgers and at Fordham. It's a beginning."

"What is your definition of happiness?"

"Waking up every morning, looking forward to the day, and knowing that something fun will happen during the course of the day."

"What were some of the happiest moments in your life?"

"My wedding day. If they had a time machine, I would like to go back to that day. It was perfect. I wouldn't have changed anything, except perhaps my shoes. It was over the Memorial Day weekend. We were about 20 friends and family members. Our wedding was very urban. We got married at City Hall, then we went to Times Square to take some pictures, had a picnic in Central Park in the afternoon, and later we went to the Village where we had dinner and went to the bars and the coffee shops. I was wearing a blue dress with a veil and carried a bouquet of flowers, and I still remember how people in the street were so happy for us and would come up to us and congratulate us."

"How would you end the sentence: 'In order to be happy, you have to…'?"

"In order to be happy, you have to like yourself, and once you like yourself, you can do good things for yourself (finding the right partner, pursuing your passions, and getting a job you like). This doesn't mean you stop working on yourself, though. Seeing myself truthfully with all my weaknesses and strengths and accepting what I cannot change but at the same time working on what you can change. I guess what it is all about is having goals, a purpose in life. When you feel good about yourself, you have energy to be good to other people, too."

Accepting my mom

Friday, 27 August

"I think happiness is being comfortable with yourself and accepting wherever you are in your life. Acceptance of self and others are key factors to happiness. I kind of went through a lot with my family. During all my teenage years, my mother was an alcoholic and I was very bitter and angry at her. But last year when I moved to the city, I found myself, and was able to accept myself and my mother the way she was. She has now been sober for five months but I feel that even if she would go back to her own ways, I would still be more accepting of her."

Kristin, sophomore in college

The joy of choosing the course of your life

Saturday, 28 August

As soon as I enter Barnes & Noble, I notice an African American lady with long grey braids and grey eyebrows. As I approach her, she looks up at me with warm, excited eyes, full of life. She is very enthusiastic about my project. Her name is Sharon.

"Getting a better relationship with God makes me happy. I do that by reading." She points at all the books in front of her. "I believe in my Holy Book. However, I am not saying that the Bible is the only truth. My husband is a Muslim. I respect others who believe in their truths.

"The second thing that makes me happy is that I try to learn about humanity, about who we are. I love people because we are all an extension of each other no matter what our background is. We all come from the same source.

"Sometimes my family—I have a daughter who is 37 and a son who is 34 years old—makes me happy but we are not as close as I would like except for my mom. She is 72 years old. I call her bionic woman because she has had a heart transplant but is still going strong. We are very close and talk very well together. You see, in my circle I don't have anybody like-minded. They all think I am 'out there.' My daughter still resents me because when she was little she went to live with the mother of her father. I was 17 years old when I got her and couldn't take care of her because I was still a child." She pauses for a while.

"I would like to become a life coach. I want people to know that your life is precious, and that they have a choice. It's a gift from God. I wish I would have known this 20 years ago but 'it isn't over until the fat lady sings' and I haven't sung yet!" She laughs.

"What happened 20 years ago?"

"From when I was nine to when I was an early teenager, I was sexually abused by my father."

"Oh! That's horrible!"

She laughs. "Oh baby! It's not as uncommon as you think! It happens all the time! I don't think that really affects my life today. I really loved my dad and was very sad when he passed away. When I grew up, we were three boys and me. One of my brothers died from a drug overdose, another from alcoholism. His liver got eaten up. So now I have only one brother left. He doesn't have a job and lives with my mom. Sometimes he will go on a drug binge for a week but he says he is only a 'social user.' Ha! My foot! I had always been drinking sporadically but when I was in my late 30s I started doing drugs on and off for three years. I felt sorry for myself. I guess I was depressed and felt without hope, that there was nothing in life for me. Then I went to rehab. I love counseling! I never went back after that! We only have one life. We have to take care of it. I firmly believe that if you don't like the way your life looks, it's the result of your choices, and that I can't blame anybody but myself. I now work in the mail room of a big company, and I meet so many interesting people there. It was nothing but God's grace!"

Sharon exudes positive energy.

"What is your definition of happiness?"

"I originally thought that happiness was when a relationship was going well. But today I think that happiness is unconditional love for everyone. I believe that this is the key to life: Love your neighbor as yourself." She smiles, and her eyes shine brightly.

"What were some of the happiest moments in your life?"

"When the lightbulbs started to go on in my head. I am 55 years old now, and in the last few months I have started to see so much clearer. I love reading self-help books. I am trying to understand why my interest has started to turn. I have always been interested in psychology and human behavior. One of the things that contributed to this was my husband, in his own strange way. He helped me to accept me for who I was. He didn't want sex because of my weight. He said he wasn't attracted to me physically but that it was my personality that he liked about me. I learnt that I had to love myself regardless of what he thought."

It is true that Sharon isn't a lightweight but you forget about that in her presence. Her love of life is contagious, and she dresses very nicely. I am admiring her electric blue tight pants, matching blue Coach sandals, the green t-shirt, and a yellow and white flowery shirt. The colors look great on her! I notice a tattoo on her neck. Large golden hoops are hanging from her ears.

"I love waking up in the morning, knowing that you have a whole day in front of you. You can choose your course. You cannot stop things from happening but you can choose how you want to respond to it.

"Life in general is another thing that makes me happy."

"How would you end this sentence: 'In order to be happy, you have to…'?"

"In order to be happy, you have to first have a relationship with your higher power, whoever or whatever that is, whatever you gravitate to or get strength from, and then love yourself. That's it! Doesn't that sound simple?" She giggles. "Why are we struggling?"

"Are you happy, Sharon?"

"I have never in my entire life been happier. I just told my mother this the other day: 'You can rest in peace here on earth and hereafter because I am very happy."

The desert

Tuesday, 31 August

"The desert makes me happy. Unless you pay close attention to a desert, you think that there is no life there and that it is never-changing. But there is a predictable change in a desert, based on the elements. Every two weeks there are new flowers that show up. When there is a rainstorm coming, you can see the shadows of the clouds on the earth because there's nothing else out there. Growing up in Los Angeles, there is a lot of desert. Looking at its vastness makes you realize how insignificant you are—at least in terms of nature."

Maya, a fellow train commuter

September

Laugh!

Wednesday, 1 September

An elderly lady with short grey hair, wearing a black and white checkered shirt and black linen pants, is reading a newspaper at a table inside the atrium of a large glass building on Fifth Avenue. I introduce myself: She seems thrilled to talk to me. Her name is Toby. I tell her I like it.

"Well, I invented it. I hate my real name: It's Thelma."

"Thelma," I repeat dreamily, "Like in *Thelma and Louise*?"

"Ssshh! Don't say it aloud! I don't want anybody to know." She laughs.

She isn't wearing any makeup nor jewelry except for a large silver watch.

"Tell me a few things that make you happy."

"To be alive—I just turned 85 years old a couple of weeks ago, and to go to museums. The most beautiful museum in the world—and I have travelled quite a bit—is the Frick Collection. You go in there, and you will be captivated by its beauty. It's packed with art from some of the most fascinating and well-known artists in the world. There is a lot of Rodin. Inside the museum there is an atrium just like this, and in its middle there is a large fountain surrounded by beautiful flowers where you can sit. It's mesmerizing. Oh! I must go there! It's my favorite place. I get a kick out of it."

"Do you go there often?"

"Well, not too often. They have increased the prices on all these museums and, you know, I live on Social Security so I have to be careful with my money.

"I also love walking and eating good food. I know every street in this city. These days I don't walk as much as I used to because although I don't use a cane, sometimes I lose my balance and I have had a few falls. Doesn't happen often but I have to be more careful.

"Laughter makes me happy. I always say that laughter is a magnificent douche. Laugh a lot and you clear all your head from worries."

She pauses. "The reason I am like I am is because I am pickled in red wine and single malt scotch. I love drinking but I moderate myself. My favorite wine is Cabernet. Recently, I have discovered some very good wines from Argentina."

"What is your definition of happiness?"

"Happiness is being me. I am happy just by being me, for the way I turned out, for the things I have done and for the things I still do. What more can I ask for?"

"What were some of the happiest moments in your life?"

"Being born."

"I assume you remember that vividly?" I ask teasingly.

"Yes, very clearly." She giggles. "I was born in Manhattan in 1925 but only weighed two pounds and one ounce. At that time there were not yet any incubators. My mother got a very special doctor, who was so intrigued with me that he made a hand-made incubator, and he even brought me to his own home, where I stayed for the first six months of my life. Thanks to him, I have never had an operation or been gravely ill in my whole life. I owe my life to him.

"Later on I moved with my parents to a large apartment in Brooklyn where I lived until I was 29, when I married. That was a big mistake. I should never have done that. You see, I am not really marriage material. But I got two beautiful sons out of it."

"Why did you marry him then, Toby? Were you in love with him?"

"I was in love with his penis. It was the biggest penis I had ever seen."

We laugh for a very long time.

"When my kids were in their early 20s, I told them it was time to go and live for themselves. I wanted to live life. I always lead a very active life: I was a tennis player, skier, handball player, and even the captain of the basketball team in high school. So when their room got freed up, I asked my husband to take the spare room, and from that time on, we basically had two separate lives. I got a boyfriend, and he did his thing. I used to love sex but for the last two or three years I have no more desires. Just the thought of it now turns me off. This worries me a little bit."

"What other happy moments do you recall fondly from your life, Toby?"

"When I began to enjoy my children and travel with them. By the time they were 16, they had been all over the world. I used to enjoy their sense of humor; they both have different ones but each of them is really funny. I never took a tour—I don't like to be led around—but went right to the country I had read up on. Arthur Frommer was my bible. I used to do my own itineraries, book bed and breakfasts, and study maps. My favorite place in the whole world is Florence in Italy. I love everything about it, even the Arnau, which is quite polluted. I have in my will that I want my ashes to be thrown in this river but the last time I was there it was so smelly that I might as well have them put in the Hudson! It's up to my boys what they do with my ashes. I don't care! I won't be here anymore." She laughs. "I don't believe in afterlife. I am an atheist. When I was a little girl, I would ask my father many questions about religion, 'Why is this so and so?' But he would only smack me and tell me, 'Because I said so.'"

"Is there a third happy moment in your life that you remember, Toby?"

"Meeting people and getting to know them. Each human being that you befriend adds to your experience and your joy."

"We have reached the last question. Are you happy?"

She looks at me mockingly, slightly tilting her head. "Do I look sad? Do I look unhappy? Is there anything about me that makes you think that I am not happy? I am happy to be alive, to eat good food, and drink good wine. I am happy to meet certain people, even you!" She winks at me.

Self-preservation
Saturday, 4 September

Today's destination, Roosevelt, is a borough in New Jersey established in 1937 during the Great Depression in order to help unemployed Jewish garment workers from New York, as part of President's Roosevelt New Deal. At the time the town had a garment factory and a farm. Most of its residents were Eastern European Jews. From an old article I had stumbled over online, I learned that Roosevelt was home to many left-wing thinkers and had attracted numerous artists.

As I drive there, I am excited at the prospect of meeting the inhabitants. However, when I park my car in front of the primary school, not a soul is in sight. No, wait! Right over there, behind the school, a man is biking. I cross the street as quickly as I can.

"Excuse me, sir," I ask him. "There used to be a deli in town. Would you happen to know where it is?"

He laughs. "That deli no longer exists. Come with me! I will show you around." He gets off his bike, and as we stroll leisurely through the township, he points out the "*bauhauses*" also called "cinder-block houses," whose roofs are totally flat, as well as the geodesic dome houses, which look like soccer balls with windows on their upper half that were built in the 1970s when there was a dome factory in town.

Since the afternoon is coming to an end, and I have not yet interviewed anybody, I ask him if he would mind answering a few questions. We sit on garden chairs outside his garage under some large trees, where he removes his shoes.

"What is your definition of happiness?"

"I think it's being at peace, not needing, and being healthy."

"How would you end this sentence: 'In order to be happy, you have to…'?"

"This might sound strange to you but in order to be happy, you have to be absolutely selfish. Taken out of context, this might seem a little bit weird. You see, you have to love yourself, and if you do that, you will not do anything that will harm yourself.

"Let me give you an example. Let's say somebody called me a name. My immediate reaction would be to insult him back but then I might suffer from a guilty feeling afterwards. If I really love myself, I should not insult him back because then I will not set up my conscience to torment me.

"Or what about this example? I am driving on a road, and suddenly somebody cuts in front of me. I get mad, I probably get an ulcer. Instead of getting mad, I should say, 'I am glad I didn't get hit,' and it in this way I love myself. You could also call it self-preservation."

"Are you happy?"

"I am usually a content person. It came with the years; I have to practice it. When something that I don't like happens, I tell myself: 'I have to preserve myself.' You won't see me jumping up and down in joy. People tell me, 'You don't show enthusiasm!' It's true but then I don't show much anger either. I think about the future and have concerns about it sometimes but I try not to let it bother me. My kids used to tell me, 'You're very boring!' And I would always reply, 'That's fine: I like it that way.'"

Be authentic to yourself
Monday, 6 September

A lady with blond hair tied in a ponytail and light golden framed glasses is reading magazines while sipping an iced drink at one of the tables in the bookstore.

"Excuse me, may I ask you a question?"

She looks up. She has pretty blue eyes and a pink t-shirt that says: "Miss Sunshine." Her name is Laura.

"How would you end this sentence: 'In order to be happy, you have to…'?"

"In order to be truly happy, you have to do a lot of soul-searching and identify what your real passions are. Make sure that what you focus on is what really matters to you. You have to understand your desires, stay on that path, and don't let anything nor anybody lead you astray. In short, I would say just make sure you are being authentic to yourself. Personally, I have a relentless desire to be honest with myself."

"What is your definition of happiness?"

"Happiness is ever evolving but it is not something that just happens. A lot of it has to do with conscious living and choices. I think that as a working mother, at this point in my life—I am now 42 years old—I have reached a time of reevaluation when I ask myself the following questions: 'What are my authentic desires? What would it take to reach them? After my family has been taken care of, what passions should I follow? Could I be pushing myself more, and what would that look like?' I think that fulfillment comes from satisfying other needs that are not necessarily monetary. I am very cognizant that our lives are passing. Once I turned 40, I was no longer that young, fresh-faced, naïve person. I want to make active, conscious choices. It's a tremendous responsibility. To me, it is very important to account for how my time is being used, and I think that it is totally connected to happiness."

Be part of the flow
Thursday, 9 September

Paula, an Argentine friend, and I are driving home after attending the opening of a painting exhibit in Manhattan. It is late in the evening, and I can barely make out her profile in the darkness of the car. Once in a while headlights of passing vehicles light up her long, silver, tear-shaped pendants, chestnut shoulder-length hair, and bottle-green dress.

"Paula, tell me three things that make you happy."

She smiles. "The sun in my face and my feet in the wet grass in the morning. It's the feeling that I am awakening with the natural world. The sun, the wet grass, and the fresh morning air make me feel that I am part of a whole, and it keeps on moving. This forces me to understand that we are just a little particle of the world, and that we are given this chance to be here. All other things fade in comparison with these."

"What is your definition of happiness?"

"Happiness is that feeling that everything is in perfect balance and that we get the chance to contribute to it all the time every day. If you think of it, to realize this, is such a blessing. That alone gives me happiness."

Such peace, energy, and joy emanate from Paula, and I wish for a traffic jam so we can extend our conversation.

"Are you happy, Paula?"

"Yes," she turns toward me and smiles. "I must add that I spent three to four years being quite unhappy, and I have worked very hard to reconnect with those elements that I identify with happiness. To me, a very basic element of this happiness that helps me to face the world is the love from my family, and in the last years my husband and our dog.

"It was the fact that I had to live with my own demons that allowed me to see that happiness is a choice. We all see things out there that make you happy or not. It's up to you to make a decision as to what you want to see. I changed my attitude.

"I had become very anxious; the things I wanted to happen were not happening, of course. I stopped seeing the little things that made me happy every day. The turning point came when something inside me said I had reached rock bottom and it was time to get up. In the past I was always pushing so hard, taking care, moving on: My happiness came from things that were happening outside me. Now I allow myself to feel, and try to let things unfold by themselves. Now I am happy from inside."

"Is there something else you would like to add on the topic of happiness?"

"You know, the other day I was listening to a well-known Chilean psychologist. She told the story of how she once got a visit from a blind person who wanted to cure his depression. She told him, 'Come back in one week, and make a list of the things that make you happy.' He did as he was told, and one week later he showed up in her office with three books full of notes. She started reading what he had written: 'These things make me happy: the smell of toast in the morning, the warm water in the shower, the softness of the towels.' She had to stop reading and started crying. The blind man asked her why she was crying. 'You just made me realize how depressed I am that I no longer see the small, happy things in life.'"

Even diamonds start out as coal

Friday, 10 September

"I try to have happy moments every day. Meeting new people. Learning new skills or something about myself. I used to decorate my classroom with small, motivational sayings. Two of my favorites are: 'What have you done today that has made you better than yesterday?' and 'Even diamonds start out as coal.' I believe that every person has a talent and that it should be developed, exposed, and shared with everyone because if everybody did what truly made them happy and what they were good at, what wrong would there be in the world?"

Don, 27 years old

Happiness can be deceiving

Saturday, 11 September

It is late afternoon when I get to Barnes & Noble. After having been declined by two people, I am happy when John, a man in his mid-50s, agrees to be interviewed.

"I am not sure I am the right person to speak about happiness. You see, my wife died of cancer. This November it will be two years."

I feel that John needs to talk so I listen to him for a long time while he shares his views on food, medicines, and the medical health care system. I then redirect the conversation toward happiness.

"What is your definition of happiness?"

He sits back in his chair and smiles. He has a warm smile and kind, albeit sad, eyes.

"I think real happiness is when you are 70 or 80 years old and you sit back on the couch because you cannot walk anymore, and you look back at your life and are able to tell yourself, 'Yes, my life was happy.'"

"Tell me some of the happiest moments in your life."

He reflects for a bit. "There were many happy moments in my life, such as when children were progressing, graduating, etc….I think one of the happiest moments was when my family joined me in the United States.

"I grew up in Poland. I was in my mid-20s when my mother died. Prior to her death, she and my father had planned to join a trip organized by a Polish priest to go to the Vatican to see Pope John Paul II. Since she passed away, my father asked me if I would come with him instead. I agreed but told him that I would not return to Poland but try to get a visa to go to the United States. I had just finished my military service and wasn't quite sure I would get a passport. However, the secret service played some game and gave everybody passports except for the priest. Life was horrible under the Communists! I spent five months in Italy before I was granted political asylum in the United States. Then I got my Green Card, and my family was finally able to join me. I was 27 years old. That was a very happy day.

"When I look back at my life, I see that many things that at the time seemed to be indicators of happiness, such as buying a house, were not really happy moments. I realize how naïve I was. Just think of the curse it is these days to own a house in the current housing market! People place too much value on materialistic things."

"How would you end this sentence: 'In order to be happy, you have to...'?"

"I know it might sound a little bit presumptuous but I would say, 'In order to be happy, you should not be ignorant but learn the truth.' But when you learn the truth, it makes you sometimes a little bit less happy because the truth can be cruel. You have to decide whether you want to be a little bit happy and ignorant, or know the truth and be less happy. There is something called 'luck,' and I think it's easier for those people who have 'luck' to be happier than others."

"I have one final question: Are you happy?"

"I have had a lucky life in which there was more happiness than unhappiness."

"Do you have any additional words you would like to add to the topic of happiness?"

"People think that they are much happier today than 50 or 200 years ago. I don't know if this is necessarily true. If we look at the history of Poland, until 1811 people were slaves. Could they be happy? I don't think so. The point is we believe we are happier today because we are free. Well, we are not free today."

Relish being able to breathe
Sunday, 12 September

Some years ago on a sunny afternoon, I had searched for a tennis partner who would play a set with me. This is how I met Al, my Jewish friend, originally from Belgium. He was five years old when the war broke out and lived in hiding for five years. He has written a moving memoir of this period of his life. Today he is my "happiness date" at an Italian restaurant.

"Al, name a few things that make you happy."

"When I am looking for something around the house to help me fix something, and I find something I have saved for 40 years that I know I should have thrown out a long time ago but which is exactly what I need to finish a certain project. When I have saved 17 cents, thanks to these long-forgotten missing pieces, I am deliriously happy. It's not the money but it's the notion that I shouldn't waste anything. Part of the deliriousness comes from how hard I laugh at myself, and the summation is, 'You see, you were right to save that object!' Of course, this happens much more often than any normal person would believe.

"One of the courses I teach is reading, a course that I have developed myself. Part of the process is that the student has to read a whole book in English, then write a book report. Besides that, the student has to give an oral report at the end of the semester. One year I had an 18-year-old lady from the Dominican Republic in my class. She gave a mediocre written report but she elected to tell the class why she had chosen the particular book she read. 'I had never read a book in my life and didn't know how to start. So I went to my aunt who had many books, and she gave me a book. Now I will buy a book.' When I heard her say these words, I wept openly in the classroom because she justified on many levels my existence as a teacher. This was an extremely happy moment in my life because I realized that I had facilitated helping kids read, report, and talk about a book. These kinds of experiences make me feel that I am contributing to society."

I look at my friend across the table. He is quick to smile. His wild-looking white hair and long whiskers frame blue, intelligent eyes and an eagle nose. He balances his glasses in his hand.

"What is your definition of happiness?"

"I think happiness is to recognize one's own mediocrity. To be happy would be to accept the result of one's own mediocrity. One should know that this is how much I can do and then, come hell or high water, be happy with the result. In this way you will learn how and who you really are, and then you can be happy with what you do or don't do.

"I also think that happiness is a figment of our own imagination. Happiness doesn't really exist, in the same way there is no such thing as time. It is the result of something you elect to believe as a consequence of something that happens to you or that you do. It's all very momentarily. We make up these things as we go along, and if they succeed, we are happy. Happiness only exists after we have put up a whole set of pre-conditions. Let's take an example. You might go and play tennis with only the goal of winning in your mind. You win, you are happy; you lose, you are unhappy. If you go to the match, thinking 'I will enjoy this whether I lose or win,' you will be happy no matter how the match turns out.

"Can anybody else make you happy? No, only if you want them to. I believe in randomness. We are all here very accidentally. Human conditions allow us to adapt so we become the king of the hill."

"Do you believe in an afterlife, Al?"

"No, I believe that this is it. Once I learned that I am not here for a reason, that there was no purpose for me being here, it made me relax much more in life. I have always been responsible but the realization that there is no purpose for me being here has made me more responsible. It made me create a purpose for myself, to be a decent fellow human being, and to be an acceptable guest on this earth. If there were a higher purpose or God, my responsibility would decrease and be limited. But if there is no higher purpose, I have to decide myself on my purpose, which gives me more responsibility."

"Al, how would you end this statement: 'In order to be happy, you have to...'?"

"In order to be happy, you have to aim for goals that you can attain."

"Al, are you happy?"

"Yes, for the most part I am. I relish the thought of being able to breathe."

Take life day by day
Monday, 13 September

A Chinese gentleman is sitting alone near the window in one of the cars of the train. By the time I sit down he is almost napping. At some point he opens his eyes. It would have been really nice to interview him…

"Excuse me, sir, may I ask you a question?"

His name is Ah, 85 years old, who has short grey hair, a tanned complexion, and is wearing a grey suit.

"Ah, tell me three things that make you happy."

"For me, at my age, to have good health and the happiness of my family are the most important things in my life. I have a wife, one daughter, one son, one granddaughter, and two grandsons."

"What were some of the happiest moments in your life?"

"I don't really have any moments that are happier than others. I am happy every day. Now that I am retired, I don't have to worry about anything. I don't think too much. I take day by day."

"Is there anything else you would like to add on the topic of happiness?"

"I am happy. What more would I have to add?" he says smilingly. "I am a very simple man. I don't envy anybody. I have what I have: You don't like my house? That is fine. You don't have to come and visit me. I try to do my best to help when I can. If I cannot afford it, I say so. I want to die healthy. I don't want to die in a nursing home. I have lived long enough now but I am still happy to walk around."

My dad

Thursday, 16 September

After having been turned down twice, I am relieved when Jason, a 33-year-old man from Ecuador with short brown hair, a hint of a mustache, and lively eyes, agrees to share a happy moment from his life.

"My parents split when I was five but I would still see my dad frequently. Every year he would spend the 31st of December with us: He would always show up around 9 p.m. I remember that one year, this was way before everybody had a cell phone, nine o'clock came and no Dad was to be seen. Nine-thirty, ten o'clock came and went. It was 10:30 but not for a second did I lose faith; I knew he would come. The clock struck 11 p.m. I started worrying: 'Where was he?' When that doorbell finally rang at 11:30, I felt that my heart was going…I knew that my dad would never let me down, that he would always do whatever he could to make my sister and me happy. I remember feeling 'I knew it!' And the fact that I could rely on him made me so happy."

I sense the emotion in his words. "Did he live up to these expectations?"

"I can honestly tell you from the bottom of my heart that I had the best dad in the world. He did not have a lot of money and worked as a shipment clerk, standing on his feet all day, but that was just irrelevant. He was always happy, very loving and hugging, teaching us what was right and wrong. Of course, there was discipline—it wasn't easy to raise kids—but there was always a lot of love. Love is important."

"Is he still alive?"

"Yes, he is. He now lives in a nursing home because, due to his diabetes, he had both knees amputated and has to sit in a wheelchair. I am sure he has his sad moments but every time I go to visit him he is so happy and always laughs. Not long ago I told my father, 'I hope that when I have children I can just be half as good a dad as you were. You did everything you possibly could for us.'"

We both get teary-eyed, and for a few moments we're not saying anything.

Happiness as a by-product
Friday, 17 September

"Happiness is the wrong thing to pursue. It should not be a goal in itself but a by-product, which comes from taking the attention off yourself, working on something meaningful, expressing your talents, skills, passions, and being used by something that is a little bit greater than yourself. If you aim for happiness, you will always be disappointed and dissatisfied. But if you aim to contribute and to make a difference, it will come naturally."

Jennifer, customer at bookstore

My son's laughter

Sunday, 19 September

A lady with short gray hair is sitting with a teenager at a table at the local library doing a puzzle depicting farm animals. Sometimes the boy puts down a piece, not realizing that it doesn't fit among the other pieces, but he keeps trying.

I have barely introduced my project before she says, "I would love for you to interview me, if this is your question."

Her son is very interested in my notepad so we ask him to write his name on one of its pages. His writing is large and scribbly but after a few hesitations and some encouraging words from his mom, he finally finishes all of the letters.

"Maybe I can ask the first question to your son, and you can help me understand three things that make him happy."

She smiles at him; he tilts his head and grins back.

"The sound of people's laughter makes him happy. He also has the best laugh I have ever heard. He loves exploring places anywhere; he is the only person I know who experiences the New York City subway as a thrill ride. He likes to play all kinds of games and to participate in all sorts of social events."

As she speaks, her son observes her and sometimes caresses her face or arms. He looks intermittently at me while grinning widely. There is something very refreshing and touching about him.

"He is a child who radiates happiness. He has a lot of special needs but he really finds joy in helping other people in any way he can. When we are visiting at Grandma's house, after a meal he will take her by the sleeve to the sink where they wash the dishes together. If she is in the kitchen and he is in the basement, he runs upstairs to help when he hears the water in the kitchen start to run. He holds doors for strangers. He helps me with daily chores and errands.

"Our speech therapist encouraged learning sign language. The sign for happiness is this." She places her hand on her stomach and rubs it upwards. He copies her. "This is the sign for sadness." Immediately, the boy draws near and draws tears on her cheeks with his fingers. "He has been able to learn quite a few words this way, although sometimes his lack of coordination skills makes them imperfect. But I can understand, and it makes me happy that we have this connection.

"All I am trying to do is to be a good mom, and I am trying to raise my son as a gentleman. We meet a lot of people, and many of them only see his special needs and quickly label him as a problem. To me, the greatest happiness is when they accept him as the young man he is, and do not act narrow-mindedly."

Suddenly, her husband appears so it is time for her to leave. "I will email you my answers to your remaining questions," she says graciously. A couple of days later, she writes to me.

"What is my definition of happiness?

"I learned to read and to love words at an earlier age than I can remember, and I have also spent many years studying all sorts of languages so I always begin with the dictionary. I like etymology: the roots from which meanings have grown and changed. One of the Latin terms for happiness is '*felicitas*,' or luck. For me, then, in a sense happiness means feeling lucky.

"Another definition of happiness for me is 'a sense of satisfaction.' By that I mean that I feel happy whenever I not only have enough but have enough to share.

"Happiness, I think, also means a feeling of completion because whenever I can finish something that I set out to do or think or say, I gain the freedom to let that piece of me go, which brings peace—a sense of order and balance, even if it doesn't last for long.

"And as my remarkable father, who lived past the age of 90, often quoted (a line from the movie *Bridge on the River Kwai*): 'Be happy in your work.' When I get discouraged by the amount of work and chores and unpleasant surprises that fill my most hectic days, I try to repeat that advice to myself, too."

"In order to be happy, you have to…"

"I believe I must seek happiness out, and I also must choose it when possible. Happiness can be a collection of little things but for me, seeking it and choosing it turn ordinary days and moments into extraordinary, memorable ones."

"Are you happy?"

"Yes. Happiness is simply a declaration of 'Yes!' And it is a possibility in infinite supply."

"Anything you would like to add to happiness?"

"Yes—more of it, a daily gift to every person on earth.

"You also asked me to try to describe three of my happiest memories:

"1. My husband's marriage proposal. His romantic idea was to hand me a Hallmark card on an ordinary weekday evening. A science-fiction enthusiast who had introduced me to author Robert Heinlein, inside the card he had written an excerpt from Heinlein's *Time Enough for Love*: 'You want it formal? All right, here's a short one, binding—and later you can have any ritual you want...Till the stars grow old and our sun grows cold? Will you fight for us, lie for us, love us—and let us love you?' I said 'Yes!' and now, years later, I'm certain that I've made at least one right choice in my life.

"2. Always, always the sound of my son's laughter. One day when he was still a small baby, he sat propped up by pillows on the couch while my husband gently tossed toward him a soft, cloth ball that had a tiny bell sewn inside. Instead of landing on the cushion beside him, the ball bounced on my son's head, which caused him to laugh delightedly for the very first time I can remember. I managed to snap a photo of the moment, and I'll always cherish that image. As the artist Brian Andreas once wrote, 'The first time his laughter unfurled its wings in the wind, we knew that the world would never be the same.' So true!

"3. Each time I take a trip to a library. I still remember the excitement I felt at the age of five when printing my name on my very first library card. I've known the Franciscan beauty of Friedsam Memorial Library and its view of '[Thomas] Merton's Heart'; I had the privilege of studying and working in Princeton University's Firestone Library and recently I received the marvelous gift of a private tour of the Grolier Club library rooms. I love libraries—they are my sanctuaries whenever I need them.

"Hope that I haven't bored you with too many details!"

Teaching
Tuesday, 21 September

"I love to teach. I taught in Kentucky, New Mexico, Guam, and New Jersey. In Kentucky, I taught migrant children (pre-k). I think they taught me more Spanish than I taught them English! They were mostly children of the workers in the onion fields. They would be three to four years old, and we used play dough and read stories (mostly picture books) but they would only stay a couple of months; the parents would move according to the crops that needed harvesting: lettuce, chilies, pecans, and apples. Some would also to go California to harvest oranges."

Rosemarie, customer at bookstore

Be engaged in life
Wednesday, 22 September

"In order to be happy, you have to be at peace, in balance, and have a variety of interests. You have to be interested and sincerely care about the world around you and in other people. You really need to be engaged to be happy, learn, and keep things fresh."

Pete, customer at bookstore

Choose a happy lens
Thursday, 23 September

"Happiness depends on what you focus on. Everybody has a lens through which they look at the world. You choose your own way, whether you choose a positive approach or a negative approach."

Danielle, studying to be a youth pastor

Self-transformation
Friday, 24 September

A man with a long grey ponytail, white mustache, and goatee, wearing a grey cap to which are attached some sunglasses, is reading at one of the tables at the bookstore. His name is Steve, and he seems very happy that I have landed in such an impromptu way at his table. After answering a few questions about the project, it is my turn to interview him.

"What is your definition of happiness?"

He remains silent for a while. "Happy, happy, happy," he repeats as if tasting it, "happy is a strange word. A little bit like 'have a nice day.' It's related to a feeling of expansiveness. It's the opposite of anxiousness. Pain and misery are a contraction within yourself. When you are emotionally expanding, you reach out to the world. Happiness is also being in contact with the world around me."

"Name one of the happiest moments in your life."

His face gets suddenly illuminated, followed by a shadow of doubt.

"I had a mystical experience in my life. It was a pivotal, very intense, expansive experience but it's really hard to describe. I was a late teenager and found myself in school studying accounting—my father was a businessman—but I just couldn't do it. Up to that day my life sort of happened. I just reacted. When I looked at the books, I got sick. I developed a type of academic anxiety. I started an existential angst and questioned what the purpose of life was. This led me to studying religion and philosophy. I dropped out of school and got a job as a bill collector but I kept thinking about this stuff. Up to that point the deepest philosophical thought that I could put together was 'everything happens for a reason.'" He laughs. "At some point I realized something, and it literally took my breath away. Basically, I plunged into a very intense ecstasy, which was at the same time emotional, physical (orgasmic), and intellectual. It was a total being experience with streaming, like pleasurable electric currents went through me. It lasted for hours. It was a strong sense of unity with all things. My brain couldn't keep up with all that was happening. It felt like an encounter with something much higher than me.

"This experience led me on a very diligent pursuit. I think that happiness has to do with a certain self-transformation that we all have to embark on. The ideal thing is to have everything, such as knowledge and being, function optimally. A great part of our work here on earth is to fix our lower centers—our emotions, physical self, and intellect—because they are all out of whack. Knowledge needs to be incorporated into who you are in order to obtain understanding. We need to be unified within ourselves. Our goal should be to get our own organisms to function in a unified manner. Only then will you be able to approach the unity that is all around you. If you are not unified within yourself, how can God even talk to you?

"In order to be happy, you have to involve your whole being in life. Otherwise, you will only be working at parts of yourself."

Contribute

Wednesday, 29 September

I notice him immediately as I enter the small café: He is probably in his early 60s with thick, white hair parted on the side, black-rimmed glasses, and reading a book at one of the tables. Anil, originally from India, tells me he is a CPA and that he himself is writing a book.

"Tell me three things that make you happy."

"Work—one of the key things to happiness is to go with your career where the heart is, helping others, and seeing younger people. I feel very optimistic when I see young people. They are willing to think outside the box, have a positive attitude, and are receptive to new ideas and changes. They are also very comfortable making alliances with people. They like to get more involved, often doing volunteer work, because they want to make the world a better place. We were brought up with hierarchies: They don't work with that structure. Titles don't mean anything to them. There are good things to come. They have a better chance of solving problems because they are open and willing to listen to others. But they need mentors, reassurance from the generation above them, and guidance so they can achieve their happiness."

"Anil, how would you end this sentence: 'In order to be happy, you have to…'?"

He rests his face in the palm of his hand. His glasses are slightly pushed up.

"In order to be happy, you have to, first of all, find peace within yourself. Each person is unique, and everybody makes a personal contribution. We have to ask ourselves: 'What is the legacy we want to leave behind? What impact will we leave the world?' For somebody to seek happiness, this is the kind of happiness you really want to seek.

"We should strive toward a spiritual happiness within ourselves, that makes us peaceful and happy but more importantly, by not making somebody else unhappy. We can call it an unselfish happiness. I am not a religious person per se but by doing good, helping others, and making a difference in the society and in the world, you get a sense that you are carrying out the orders of a superior force. I don't think I find God by going to a temple or following rituals. It's by doing these things that you will seek superior power, and you will find happiness. In a broad sense I think that happiness comes from giving more to the world than what you receive. This is genuine happiness."

"What were some of the happiest moments in your life?"

"When you find a partner that fulfills your life, somebody who is willing to go the whole ride, bad or good times. We have been married for 36 years. It feels like yesterday.

"The birth of my son and my daughter. When your children are born, two things happen: Firstly, in that instant, you realize how your parents felt about you and everything becomes clear. Secondly, for the first time in your life, you want to live for somebody. It gives you a new life and a new happiness. There is finally a purpose to you being in this world. It completes your world.

"Other happy moments take place when I had academic achievements, every time I have reached a certain landmark in my life, and I know that 'you are a better person than you were a day ago.'"

"Anil, are you happy?"

"Yes, I am happy. I think that if you don't have unrealistic expectations from life, it's easier to be happy. I also think that as I age, I become happier because I have a better understanding of the world we live in."

October

Three not so grumpy old men
Saturday, 2 October

It is mid-afternoon on one of those Indian summer days when I start kayaking up the Delaware and Raritan Canal in search of somebody to interview.

A long, wooden bridge across the river suddenly appears, and a person is standing on it, perfectly still. From a distance, I cannot make out what he is doing. As I get closer, I realize he is a photographer with a huge camera and long lenses. On another bridge nearby is yet another photographer. I greet them, continue paddling, but quickly retrace my route and return to the man with a wide-brimmed khaki hat. Although he does not want to give me his name, he agrees to an interview. I am sitting in my kayak, and once in a while I have to paddle myself back to the bridge as my boat slowly drifts away.

"Having somebody who makes me happy, and getting a perfect shot make me happy. I have been taking pictures since I was a teenager. My favorite subject is birds. You see why many of us are here today? It's to get a picture of the bald eagle. He used to have a nest not far from the lake over there but then it came down in a recent storm. Now we do not know where he nests. We saw him about an hour and a half ago." He stops and captures a photo of a flock of Canada geese flying over the bridge.

"I am a physicist and do research at Princeton, and when I get an eureka moment solving my equations, that also makes me really happy."

"What is the relationship between a physicist and a photographer?"

"You will be surprised to see how many physicists enjoy beauty because we see how the natural laws really work. When we see a rainbow or a sunset and can explain how it works, that is happiness, especially when you are the first one to discover it," he chuckles.

Sam, a fisherman in washed-out blue jeans and a white and blue shirt wearing a blue cap and glasses, joins our conversation.

"I love spending vacation time with my wife, to whom I have been married for 31 years.

"I live across the road in an apartment so another thing that makes me happy is to fish with my friends. We even come here in winter, as early as February. We put on our gloves and coats, and all the retirees come here."

"All the happy people," laughs the photographer-with-the-wide-brimmed-hat.

"Being retired makes me happy too," Sam continues. "Not having to go to work and being able to get up and go to bed whenever I feel like it. I grew up in Trenton, and we were six kids so when I was 15 years old, I started working to get pocket money and contribute to the household. I worked in the printing industry for 42 and a half years. I thank God every day for waking up, when I can put my foot on the floor. That's a good start."

"What is your definition of happiness?"

"Being around happy people. Makes the day go by nice because there is so much trouble."

"Name some of the happiest moments in your life."

"When I wake up in the morning and I can smell the coffee my wife makes in the kitchen—she makes it the old-fashioned way using a percolator—and when I go to church on weekends. They have a great service. I look forward to that."

"Sam, how would you finish this sentence: 'In order to be happy, you have to…'?"

"In order to be happy, you have to be grateful and praise God."

It is now time to interview Jim, the second photographer, so I paddle over to the other bridge.

"Hide while you can!" the photographer-with-the-wide-brimmed-hat yells over at Jim. Scenes from the movie *Three Grumpy Old Men* come to mind except for the fact that none of these men are grumpy.

Jim approaches the railing of the bridge.

"Tell me three things that make you happy."

"Laughter, especially the giggles of children. Jazz and blues music. Love."

"What is your definition of happiness, Jim?"

"Being content with what you have."

"Tell me some of the happiest moments in your life."

"When I wake up every morning and realize I am alive, and I survived the night.

"Christmases as a child. You had the anticipation of having presents. I had one sister but my mom was the biggest child. She could not wait to the 25th of December so we would always celebrate Christmas on the 24th. She loved the opening of the gifts, more than the gifts themselves, so we would never buy her one big gift but lots of small presents."

We both smile at this remembrance, while two Canada geese swim calmly by.

Suddenly, two birds soar high above the river, and Sam asks, "Is that the eagle up there?"

"No, those are vultures," Jim replies.

"No happiness yet!" adds the photographer-with-the-wide-brimmed-hat.

I look at the watch. It is almost time to return the kayak so I have to go. I thank my newfound friends for letting me interview them. We wave at each other as I paddle off in the sunset.

After a few minutes of paddling, a bagpipe starts playing on the other side of the river behind the trees. I stop rowing, let myself drift with the current, and get carried away by the music—lost in the reflection of the green and yellow leaves and the blue of the sky. Crows are croaking, casual joggers run by, and the sun is so low I can hardly see anything on the river. Just the strong rays of the setting sun. I smile to myself. "This is what true happiness feels like: these special encounters and connections along the sinuous way of this thing called life."

Life is not one long trip of happiness
Sunday, 3 October

Waiting for my son's tutoring session at the library to end, I meet Bob, 79 years old but who looks much younger. He takes me by surprise when he says, "You want to hear the most unhappy periods of my life? Life is a series of ups and downs. It's not one long trip of happiness."

I nod.

"When I got a divorce and when I lost my boy. He was 20 years old. He got a seizure, and his heart just stopped. My wife and I were married 27 years. One day she just took off and got into the women's liberation movement. I think she felt she was subservient to me and wanted her freedom. After she left, she never reached economic freedom but she never complained. I'm still paying alimony. It's not a good state."

"Thanks for sharing that, Bob. Now what about the happy moments?"

"Will this take long? I have to read *The New York Times*." He scratches his head and removes his glasses. "Well, I think when your children succeed in life and they are happy, then you are happy. My daughter had a hard time conceiving so when she got two sets of twins, those were very happy moments. Or what about when I got out of the Navy after having been there for four years? I just caught the tail of the Korean War. Or when I was accepted at Stuyvesant High School. There were about 20,000 people who applied, and they only selected about 500 to 600 of us.

"Another time was when the Brooklyn Dodgers beat the New York Yankees in the World Series. It was the first and only time they beat them. I was a rabid Dodgers fan, and I would go and watch them. Sometimes I would go with my stepdad—I lost my dad when I was eight years old but my mother remarried and I got the best stepdad anybody could get."

"How would you end this sentence: 'In order to be happy, you have to…'?"

"In order to be happy, you have to be an optimistic person, enjoy people and life. Period. It's not good to be an introvert. Treasure your friends. They are one of the most valuable things in life. Be grateful to people who are friendly to you, and you will never be bored."

"Are you happy, Bob?"

"Yes, very happy."

Visiting the Red Sox locker room
Tuesday, 5 October

Brian, a young man in his early 20s wearing a FedEx uniform, is resting on a bench. He has a calm, slightly reserved, demeanor.

"What were some of the happiest moments in your life?"

"December 2008 when my family and I went to the Dominican Republic to celebrate Christmas and New Year's together. All my family was there, and we would eat, play dominoes, listen to music, and dance.

"When I got to go to the locker room of the Red Sox in 2004. The father of one of the players was a good friend of our family so my dad took me to their locker room, and I got to meet all the players. I will always remember that day."

He seems at a loss as to what to say next.

"Brian, tell me the happiest memory from your childhood."

"I lived in the Dominican Republic until I was seven years old. We lived in the poor part of town. When I had just turned seven, I got a bike from my dad, who had moved to the U.S. This bike looked like a motorbike, and I loved it. I was the only one in my neighborhood who had a bike, and I used to ride it all the time. When I would do bad stuff, my grandma would hang it up so I couldn't ride it, and I would cry for days. I still remember this vividly."

"If I gave you one wish, what would that be?"

"I would wish to be rich to support my family."

"Do you have any comments on happiness that you would like to add?"

"I would say that just being, just living here on earth, should make us happy."

Put a smile on somebody's face
Wednesday, 6 October

Today's "happiness date" is Kofi, which means "born on Friday" in Akan, one of the languages in Ghana. He is 22 years old and studying computer engineering in the U.S.

"Happiness to me is a way of being, a state that I deliberately strive for, whereby I express myself positively in order to put a smile on my face, as well as on other people's faces, and whereby I also try to make other people happy through my actions."

"What were some of the happiest moments in your life?"

"One of the happiest moments in my life was during my teenage years when I went on an exchange program to a small town in Missouri for my senior year. It was strange to come from a large city, such as Accra, and end up in a small village of maybe 5,000 to 10,000 people. I lived with a host family, learned to know a new culture, and got friends from all over the world, with whom I am still in touch. It was hard for me to return to Ghana after that year abroad because I felt that I no longer fitted in. In my country people tend to stick with those who belong to the same economic status as yourself. In the States I had friends from a wide spectrum on the social scale. It was difficult to adapt to my old friends' way of thinking but this allowed me to weed out my bad friends from the good friends.

"Other moments I remember with fondness were when I was in high school in Ghana. Every year we would celebrate something called UNICEF day: On this day we would usually get off, and the students were invited to participate in all kinds of activities organized by NGOs. One of these activities was to make 'Happy Mother's Day' cards for the mothers of the homeless children. First, we would sit with the kids and make the cards, then we would get the cards, put some money in them, and return them to the children. When they smiled at me, that made me really happy."

"Kofi, are you happy?"

He hesitates for a moment. "As human beings, no matter what we achieve or accomplish, we will always face challenges in life. However, one thing that really makes me happy, in spite of our adversities, is simply to breathe. If I had to pay for every time I breathe, I couldn't do it. I am living, I am not disabled, and I can walk around. Many people would wish to have what I have."

Fishing
Thursday, 7 October

Nick, a 52-year old colleague, and I are sitting on a bench in the shade of a large tree in a park near work.

"Tell me three things that make you happy."

"The things I get to do in my free time. I am an avid fisherman. It stems back to when I was a kid. I was born and raised in Manhattan but on the weekends my dad would drive us to Jones Beach, where my older brother would swim and I would fish. When I was seven or eight years old, we would drive to the Catskills, and I learnt about rivers and lakes. I loved nature. On my seventh birthday I got a fishing rod, and I have not stopped since then.

"I teach fly-fishing. I also taught my partner how to fly-fish, and we make sure we go fly-fishing for two to three weeks every year. We even spent one week in a little outpost in Lappland (Sweden) for eight days. It was fantastic!

"The happiest times in my life are when I am standing in my waders in a fairly remote area where you cannot hear the hustle and bustle of the cars, just the natural sounds. It changes my demeanor. New York City keeps you on edge. Fishing is a relaxing experience. It's not just the fact of catching the fish but it is also about spending time in nature. If you stand still in the river for 20 minutes, you will see the most amazing things. You can see otters and beavers. This is a Zen moment: I become part of the river. It usually takes me a couple of days to get to this point. This is when I am at my happiest. In the past I used to be more focused on what I catch but now I mostly do catch and release.

"The second thing that makes me happy is my partner, Hans. We have been together for 15 years. He is Swiss and lives over there so we go and visit each other frequently. My family loves him. My nieces and nephews call him Uncle Hans. We are a bunch of rowdy Italians so sometimes it's hard for him but he has gotten used to us now."

He stops and studies the squirrels jumping on the gravel and the sun filtering through the leaves.

"How would you end this sentence: 'In order to be happy, you have to...'?"

"In order to be happy, you have to make yourself happy. I don't think that other things will make you happy. Happiness is self-prescribed. I don't always succeed. You can do things the hard way or the easy way: I try to look at the funny side of things."

"Nick, tell me some of the happiest moments in your life."

"A very happy moment was when I was selected for my job in the Staff Counsellor's office, and my volunteerism for HIV at the Gay Men's Health Crisis center for many years allowed me to work with HIV globally. Through our program UN Cares, we have been able to provide medication to UN staff members infected with HIV through the UN medical dispensaries around the world. This job has allowed me to do something positive for a lot of people. Through our example we have convinced governments that they needed to do the same for their people. Our efforts have made a real impact. Very recently, UN Cares was selected for one of the UN 21 awards. This made me really happy.

"Another very happy moment was when I caught this huge salmon on my fly rod in the Campbell River in Vancouver. That day I got 19 fish on my line, and they all took me for a ride but I only landed two. The others broke the line, and one even broke the rod. The river was running high and very fast. The salmon would go up the pools above me and then run back to the rapids, down to the pools and up the rapids again. I had to hold on for my life. It was wild. It would just jump out of the water and then land back in the water again. When I finally was able to reel it in, I was exhilarated. The high lasted for days, and I had trouble sleeping. It weighed 45 pounds. After taking a picture with it, which I had to develop the very next day, I released it back to the river."

I jot down number "3" on my notepad.

"I don't want to give you another fishing story," he says, "It's like my friends always tell me, 'Is there any photograph of you where you are not holding a fish?' I am trying to find another happy moment when I am not holding a fish."

I let him time to think.

"Of course! I have a good one: when Hans proposed to me in Davos. We had been skiing and one evening, he just went down on one knee and asked me to be his life partner. He gave me a Cartier ring and a Breitling watch, in which he had engraved the date of his proposal. We both wear the same ring and watch, which brings me to another funny story. The day I caught the 45-pound salmon, I thought I had lost my wedding band. All day long when I was fishing, I kept looking down at the grass and in the sand of the riverbank. I was quite desperate. On my way back to the hotel, I called from a diner and asked them to look for the ring in my room but they couldn't find it. When I got back to the hotel, I was really tired and looked forward to removing my waders: My foot had been hurting me the whole day from what I thought was a stone stuck at the bottom of it. 'Damn, my foot is killing me!' I slowly pulled off my waders, shook my boots, and heard a clunking sound on the floor: It was my ring! To this day the ring is still a little bit off center. Hans always laughs when he sees it."

"Nick, are you happy/"

"Sometimes. I won't say all the time. I am more happy than I am unhappy. My job can sometimes get to me. It reminds me that there is a lot of suffering out there but it also gives me a different perspective on things: You have to enjoy the moment and live in the present, not just look forward to that happy day because you don't know if it will ever happen."

"Nick, how would you end this sentence: 'In order to be happy, you have to…'?"

"I think you have to remind yourself all the time, when you feel the blues coming on, that we are so lucky we have everything. You have to find things that give you peace within yourself and make a real effort to make yourself positive, not negative. If not, you will only bring yourself down."

Fear is the mind killer

Saturday, 9 October

It has been a great tennis match with many long, challenging rallies. When we finish, I ask Britta if she would mind being interviewed. She agrees. We sit down on a nearby bench.

"Happiness is when I do things that make me feel like me. When I am completely being my best self and true to myself, that's when I am the happiest."

"In order to be true to yourself, you have to have found yourself. How do you do that?"

She smiles and reflects for a while. "One of my favorite quotes is from the Tao Te Ching, and it has become a mantra to me. It goes like this: 'Hold on to the center.' If you hold on to what's at the center of you (your qualities) and if you don't stray far from that, that's how you know who you are. When I feel lost, hurt, or challenged, I go back to my center, and I hold on to it; it reminds me of who I am, and I feel ok."

"Name a few happy moments in your life."

She bites her lip and looks out over the tennis courts. An owl is gliding majestically over us against the setting sun.

"One of them was when I was hiking with a bunch of friends in Virginia. My ex-boyfriend, who had just broken up with me, was in that crowd, too. He had been my first love. It was slightly awkward. One day he and I left the others behind, and did a very challenging trek up a mountain. We got to the top, where there was a big, flat black rock that had been warmed by the sun. I remember lying down on this hot rock, feeling the heat warming me from below, and the sun warming me from above. The view over the Shenandoah Valley was breathtaking. I just remember thinking, 'Forget about him. The world is so beautiful, and I am so happy.' This was one of these moments when you realize that happiness comes from within, not from another person.

"When my husband and I first started dating we went to Iceland. We had only been dating for a couple of months so we didn't know each other very well. I did not know that my husband-to-be would get really grouchy when he got hungry, and he didn't know that, for me, dinner is always very important. One night we couldn't make up our minds to find a suitable place to eat, and we got into our first fight.

We ended up going to this hotdog stand, which was the most famous hotdog place in Iceland. It even had a picture of Bill Clinton eating a hotdog there. They were the grossest hotdogs I had ever eaten. My husband inhaled his in a heartbeat. I took one bite of mine, then spit it out. We both started laughing uncontrollably. We learned how to fight that day, and how to laugh it off. I learned not to let him get hungry, and he learned to make sure I always get a good dinner."

"Is there anything you would like to add to the topic of happiness?"

"I think that fear is mostly what sucks happiness out of people. When I look at my problems in the past, they almost always stem from fear. Fear is the enemy of happiness. Letting go of fear is the key to being happy. I will mention another one of my favorite quotes: 'Fear is the mind killer.'"

When I returned from Iraq

Sunday, 10 October

Gene, a dark-haired young man with a beard who is wearing a motorcycle jacket with his black helmet resting on the table in a coffee shop, is today's "happiness date." He is studying to be a history teacher, after having spent six years in the U.S. Marine Corps and two years in Iraq.

"Tell me three things that make you happy."

"Freedom in general, the ability to be self-sufficient and to be dependent on as few things as you can, having good relationships with others, and the pursuit of knowledge. The more you can know, the better. I like to learn about everything: the existence itself, how the universe works."

"What were some of the happiest moments in your life?"

"The day I came back from Iraq and saw my family again after one year."

I write down a number two on the page waiting for his next answer.

"You want another one? It's going to be very hard to top that one!" he smiles. "Living on my own, being on my balcony, having a barbeque with friends."

"Is there anything else you would like to add to the topic of happiness?"

"I think that in order to be happy, you should not take anything too serious, especially not yourself. I learned this in Iraq, and I believe this is what saved me. My motto would be: 'Nobody is shooting at me, life is good!'"

My Family in Pakistan

Friday, 15 October

Mohammad is my friend from Afghanistan who has a fruit stand close to where I work. He is tall, slim, and has a mustache. He is resting on a windowsill of the nearby store and smiles at me as I approach him. I tell him about my book and ask if he would mind being interviewed.

"I don't speak English so well. You might not understand me."

"Let's try!" I say optimistically. "Tell me three things that make you happy."

I am not quite sure he understands me, or if he knows exactly what to answer. An African American lady passes by, grabs his hand teasingly, and answers, "Money, Mohammad! Money will make you happy! And women!"

"Sure, money makes me happy. When you don't have money, there are many things you cannot get. If you have money, you can just go in a store and say, 'Give me this, give me that one.' If you don't have money, you just look at things and never buy." He sighs. "My family makes me happy. When I was a young man, not a man," he points to his face, "and I didn't have a beard yet, I fled to Pakistan. It was just before the war with Russia. My family joined me there a few years later. Now my wife and eight kids live in Pakistan. The oldest one is 21, and the youngest one is four years old. I only have one wife. In Pakistan, I have a small business where we sell textiles."

I look down at Mohammad's colorful fruit stand: nectarines, small boxes of nuts, apples, grapes, bananas, blueberries, raspberries, and even small decorative pumpkins. Once in a while we get interrupted by customers. Mohammad greets everybody warmly and wishes them a good weekend when they leave. When he is done attending them, he returns to me.

"Have you always sold fruits?"

"No, I have had a lot of different jobs. When I first came here, I worked in construction. I also sold belts and shish kebabs. Now I have been selling fruits for three years."

"Mohammad, is there a third thing that makes you happy?"

He thinks for a while. "My religion. Thank God that I am a Muslim. Judaism came first, then Christianity, and at the end Islam. I think that's the best religion. When I pray, my heart feels relaxed, my body calm, and I am happy."

"Tell me some of the happiest moments in your life."

"Life is very different here. I cannot tell you. You should go to India, Pakistan, and Afghanistan and do interviews over there. You would get a lot of stories for your book."

"Are you afraid I wouldn't understand?"

"I have a lot of stories about how I fled Afghanistan, went to Pakistan, and then to this country. But I don't speak English well and wouldn't be able to tell you these stories. I like this country. It's a good country but things have changed. I don't have any problems with anybody. I don't fight with anybody. That's it."

I sense that he is getting guarded, and I don't want to insist.

"Are you happy, Mohammad?"

"Thank God I am happy but I would be happier with my family. I have been in the U.S. since 1991, and I have filed papers for all of them to come here. But I need somebody to co-sign for me because I don't make a lot of money so it's difficult for me to get them over here."

When I became born again
Monday, 18 October

An African American man in a grey jumpsuit, black jacket, and hat is sitting in a chair overlooking a colorful stand selling ties, hats, scarves, and gloves. He is eager to talk to me about happiness.

"In order to be happy, you need to have a relationship with your Creator. He created everybody. So in order to be content, you need to connect deeply with Him."

"What were some of the happiest moments in your life?"

"Whenever I can bring somebody to the Lord, whenever they become born again, is always a big moment in my life. I particularly remember this one fellow that I knew. He had been into drugs and was carrying firearms. I always spoke to him about Jesus and brought him to church with me. One day he accepted Jesus as his Lord and Savior. He apologized to his father for any ill-doing he had done, he quit using drugs, and he let go of the weapons. Six months later he just died in his sleep. At least he died in Christ."

He stops to help a customer, then returns to his chair.

"The biggest moment of happiness, though, was when I got saved. You see, I spent close to 20 years in jail for drugs. I used to shoot it up. We used to have this minister who would come to the penitentiary sometimes. During one of his services he started singing 'Amazing grace, how sweet the sound, that saved a wreck like me. I once was lost and now I am found, I was blind and now I see.' I felt a wind that just blew through me. The man next to me cried, I started crying, and a lot of other guys who attended the service started crying, too. That day I became born again. I stopped using drugs, and when I came home again, I started going to church and have been doing it ever since—this was in 1989."

Stop worrying
Thursday, 21 October

"I think that we spend unnecessary time worrying about things, which in 95 per cent of the cases never come to fruition. Worrying will take away the happiness from us and the will to be happy. If we only could have the courage not to worry, then I think that most of us would be happy."

Masimba, colleague from Zimbabwe

Final happiness in Heaven
Saturday, 23 October

"Are you happy?"

"Working at it. Happiness is not being at the top of the world all the time. Happiness is like a journey: It's not something you own. It's the journey toward. Happiness is not tangible nor containable. It's immeasurable. There is more of it to come. Happiness is not limited until there is no more but then there will still be happiness in a way that we cannot imagine or describe. I think that final happiness comes when you are in Heaven."

Geraldine, Barnes & Noble

History books
Sunday, 24 October

Aidan's feet are dangling from the swinging bench on my porch. He is 12 years old and has light brown, curly hair and oval glasses.

"Tell me three things that make you happy."

"Football: I have been playing tackle football for the last three or four years.

"Reading history books. I got interested in reading about history when I was eight or nine years old. I especially like war history. Napoleon Bonaparte is my hero because he was a great leader who managed to conquer a lot of land and keep his country together.

"Swimming makes me happy. There is no competition. You can do whatever you want. It is a nice way to cool off on a hot summer day. It also relaxes me."

I notice that he is touching his fingers nervously while he is talking.

"What were some of the happiest moments in your life?"

"Christmas," he replies without hesitation, "Christmas is a day when everybody is happy. It's almost impossible not to be happy. Last year, me and my young brother woke up Spencer (their sister) at 3 a.m. to open our stockings, and she got so mad. At 6 a.m. we rushed into my dad's room. He slowly got out of bed, took his video camera, and we went to the Christmas tree. We always have a real tree, which all of us go to cut at the tree farm. Last year I got a hamster so I put him in a cage but he died this spring. Once I am done arranging my gifts, I take my favorite gift and play with it. At night we will have a nice dinner."

"Any other happy moments?"

"When I got 'A' in Language Arts last year, and when I go skiing and do good on a big hill. I like the feeling of wind in my face and the snow."

"Would you like to add anything about happiness?"

"Everyone deserves happiness."

Time
Monday, 25 October

"Time makes me happy. As I become older, time becomes more precious. When you are young, you don't realize how the years pass by. I guess it's because you have more time ahead of you than behind you. I don't want to live until I am 140 years old but I would like a good quality of life, and time to be with family and friends, and not to have to watch the clock constantly."

Lynn, British tourist

Be active and mingle with people
Wednesday, 27 October

On my way to the post office I notice a local Senior Citizens Center and get excited at the idea of finding somebody to interview there.

The receptionist leads me to a classroom, where a teacher is standing in front of 20 adults who are scribbling down notes as he speaks.

"This is Dr. Ingenbrandt. He comes here once a week to teach lectures about European leaders. I believe he is talking about Greece today."

I wait until the class ends and the students trickle out of the classroom, followed by Dr. Ingenbrandt. He is wearing beige khaki pants, an off-white turtleneck, and carries a large multicolored umbrella. His hair is snow white, his nose aquiline, and his blue eyes are surrounded by a pair of large, grey glasses. He gladly agrees to the interview. We sit down in two comfortable armchairs facing the window.

"Dr. Ingenbrandt, tell me three things that make you happy."

"Having a healthy, satisfied family. I have a wonderful wife, daughter, and two granddaughters, and a son-in-law who is perfect! Happiness is when I am devoted to them, and they are devoted to me.

"Having a job that you like. In my case it is teaching. I have been teaching English and German for 63 years, and I always found good in all my students. There were only two students that I didn't like.

"I think that something else that makes you happy is keeping busy, learning, and being able to travel. In my life I have made 30 trips to Europe as a tour guide. Every year, during the last week of May, I would take 30 to 40 people from this area, and we would fly to Luxembourg and board a bus. I had the same driver for 30 years, and we would tour Europe and return two weeks later.

"Respect is another point for happiness. Respect other people and they will respect you."

"How would you end this sentence: 'In order to be happy, you have to…'?"

"In order to be happy, you have to keep active, try to find the best in everyone, and have a positive attitude toward life. I think that's my motto. Happiness is when you mingle with other people. I would hate to live a lonely life."

"If you had one wish, what would that be?"

He thinks for a while. "My one wish would be to be healthy again, and to do it all over one more time. Well, actually, not everything. The reason I am correcting myself is that I would not want to be in World War II again. I put in four years in the service and served 16 to 18 months in the Pacific, where I worked in the control tower and directed big bombers (B-29). Although I never really was in the line of fire, I saw the devastation of this war, and not far from where I worked there were three huge cemeteries testifying to this war."

Dr. Ingenbrandt smiles often when he speaks and makes sure I get it all down on paper.

"Doctor, what were some of the happiest moments in your life?'

"When I found out I was going to be a father. I still remember where I was that day. I was at the Masonic Club, and all of a sudden they announced it on the loudspeaker all through the building, 'Dr. Ingenbrandt is now a father!'

"My married life. My wife and I have been married for 62 years. We have never had a fight. My wife always tells me, 'No one can get in an argument with you.' If I didn't agree, I just kept my mouth shut, and if she didn't agree, she just kept her mouth shut but we never argued."

"Don't you think it's good to argue once in a while? That the relationship can even improve after that?"

"No, I don't think so because when two people argue it's so easy to say something that you will regret later, and then it's too late.

"My happy hours were moments being with people, teaching, and travelling. The only unhappy trip I had was when I travelled to Europe for the 31st time, and I was with my two granddaughters. I had always been the leader, and this is probably one of my weaknesses: I like to be the leader, and that time I was only the traveller. I remember the guides passing statues and water fountains, and not commenting on them. I felt that the guides were not up to par, and this made me so angry."

We both laugh heartily.

"Dr. Ingenbrandt, are you happy?"

"Yes, I am happy. The only thing that disserves me is my age. Old age brings all sorts of problems. I am 87 years old, and my wife is 92 but if you saw her you would think that she was 82! I have no fear of dying. I am so satisfied. I am ready any time."

He smiles but then a shadow runs across his face. "But I am afraid of suffering. I believe that I lived in the best of ages in the history of the U.S. Our children do not have the joys we had. Of course, there were hard times in the 1920s and the 1930s when we were very, very poor and yet we were very happy. We lived in a nice neighborhood where people looked out for each other. I ultimately believe that being happy is making other people happy."

It is never too late
Friday, 29 October

"I love your outfit!"

An African American lady with short hair, wearing a nurse's uniform from the 60s with a little cape and a dark-blue beret with a red cross, looks up at me from the floor of the bookstore, where she is sitting reading a book. A white underskirt is sticking out from under her navy-blue skirt. She wears black high-heeled shoes. Her name is Erica. When asked what makes her happy, she is prompt to answer.

"I like to help others. It lifts me out of my blue mood. I am dressed up like this because I am going to volunteer at a hospital for children in the Bronx for Halloween. We will have a party, pass out treats, and sing songs. You see, I decided to dress up as a nurse because I know what it is to be afraid of nurses and doctors. When I was six years old, my parents decided that it was time for me to get my tonsils out—that was the modern medicine of the 60s for you—and I was very scared. I remember my parents, trying to cheer me up, brought me to the zoo the day before the operation, and I remember falling in love with the monkeys. This was the first and last time my parents took me to the zoo, and I was happy just to have my parents all to myself. I also have two sisters. The next day the doctor took out my tonsils at a top children's hospital. Still, I was very fearful of the operation. I remember waking up crying. The good thing was that I could eat a lot of ice cream and watched Betty Boop on television. That's why I have this Betty Boop bag with me today."

Erica smiles often, and she exudes life. "Children make me happy. I wasn't blessed with them but I love them, and besides being a case worker, I am also a tutor. You see, when I was a case worker for kids in foster care, I would very often feel helpless so I am studying to be a paralegal. I would like to become a lawyer and advocate for children. I am 55 years old; I am taking baby steps, and it might take me eight or nine years. As a child, I didn't have anybody to encourage me. Twenty years ago I wanted to study to become a lawyer, but everybody told me, 'You are too old,' 'The market is no good,' and 'You are not smart enough.' But now I don't give a dam. I am alone now, my parents are dead, I don't have any husband to hold me back—I had a very bad marriage but now that is over—and no kids. This is my chance! I want to study in California because I have heard that over there they are very supportive of older women who want to study."

November

The happiness of being free
Wednesday, 3 November

An African American lady with lots of curly, brown hair is reading a small novel at the café at the bookstore. Her name is Fatou, and she is from the Gambia.

"Nanga def?" I ask. This means "how are you" in Wolof, one of the main languages in West Africa.

She laughs heartily. "Where did you learn that?"

"From my Senegalese friends. I travelled around in Senegal and the Gambia for three weeks. They are beautiful countries."

We chat for a while before starting the interview.

"To me, happiness is being independent," she states. "I am divorced and able to do things my own way and at my own time."

"I guess it's easier to be independent here than back home."

"Yes," she nods, "it's easier here. When you get married in Africa, you get married to the whole family. They all blamed me for the divorce and told me, 'He is such a nice man, good father, and provider.' But they were not in my shoes and didn't know what he did to me. I simply couldn't stay with him. After 30 years of marriage, I walked in on him and his mistress in my bed. It was just unbelievable! It was like he was trying to kill me. He was the man I fell in love with, the first man in my life. He pursued me for two years before I finally agreed to marry him. I kept telling him, 'I know your kind. You are a womanizer.' I finally gave in and married him, and this is what happened. I moved out shortly after this happened. I didn't want any of his money nor the things that had been in the apartment. I gave most of it to the Salvation Army. Phew! I didn't want to be near anything she might have touched! We had a joint savings account that we both had contributed to: I didn't take any of the money. I make my own money and can support myself. We have been divorced for many years now.

"My ex-husband keeps contacting me and asks for us to get married again but I am afraid I would not have any peace of mind if I went back to him, always worrying about his whereabouts and if he was faithful to me. I still love him but, with my high blood pressure, would it be wise to return to him and have to worry every day?

"My dad always used to tell me, 'Never let a man hit you or make your life miserable. Never think you cannot make it by yourself.'"

Making cakes

Friday, 5 November

A beautiful African American lady is flicking through pages with colorful pictures of a cookbook in the café at the bookstore. When asked if I can interview her, she seems hesitant at first.

"You are catching me at a little bit strange moment because I just had a big fight with my husband. I will try to get back into a happy mood," she laughs.

Robyn is wearing a cream-colored turtleneck with a bottle-green cardigan wrapped around her with a wide, black leather belt. Beautiful light pink earrings match a similar long necklace. She has a wonderful smile.

"My husband makes me happy most of the time. We have been together for five years but we only got married one year ago."

"What do you like most about your husband?"

"He's just really helpful. He cooks, cleans, and is very supportive of me. I got a promotion not long ago, and he would prepare mock interviews for me. I know I can always count on him and that whatever project we have to do, we will always do it together. It's a very big difference from how I grew up, where my father never helped." She pauses. "Cookbooks make me happy. Sometimes just reading about food, how to prepare it, and looking at the pictures makes me happier than actually making it, getting dirty, and having to clean up everything afterwards. I particularly love making cakes and decorating them. I have taken a few classes and done very fancy things, even paid work for people." She takes out her iPhone. "Look! This is one of my cakes!" She shows me a beautiful chocolate torte covered with chocolate ribbons and raspberries in the middle, as well as a coconut cupcake tower. "In my mind it's my retirement career. I do a lot of baking, especially with the holidays coming up. The other day I did a brown butter pumpkin layer cake that came out really good."

We say goodbye and promise to email each other recipes the following week.

When I come home, my sweet dough has risen to perfection, and I finalize a delicious braided cake filled with homemade vanilla custard and applesauce.

Give gifts to people

Monday, 8 November

Raindrops are falling heavily on my windshield, and I have to drive slowly. Judging from the destitute house in this run-down area of Trenton where soup kitchens and day centers for homeless abound, I sense that it is not the safest of areas. Suddenly, in a corner under the bowed entrance of a church, I notice the silhouette of a woman sitting alone, holding her hands between her legs to keep warm. I make a U-turn and park the car.

As I walk up the stairs toward her, she looks at me suspiciously.

"Hi, my name is Elisabeth. What's your name?"

"I am Catherine."

She is wearing worn white sneakers, jeans, and a white winter jacket that reaches her knees. Her hands are covered with black woolen gloves. Her auburn hair is partly hidden by the hood of her jacket.

"I am writing a book on what happiness means to people. Would you be willing to answer some questions?"

She has been listening attentively but now sadness shadows her face again. "This is not really a great day for me. I don't feel too good today. I am homeless, you see."

"I am truly sorry to hear that. How long have you been homeless?"

"For two months. I used to be a waitress at a very good restaurant. Then I lost my job, and it's so hard to find a job out there. Maybe we could do this another time?"

"Well, I work in the city. I don't really come down here very often."

My disappointment must have been very noticeable. She looks straight in front of her for a while, then adds. "Ok, what are your questions?"

"Tell me three things that make you happy."

"Have peace and quiet, not too many people around me, but those that I like to be around have to be honest, caring, and straightforward. I enjoy giving gifts to people and seeing them smile. I like doing stuff for others. When you see that glow on their faces, that makes me really happy."

I look around her little dwelling. In an opposite corner leftover food, a can of soda, and a yellow winter coat are laying on the floor. She follows my gaze.

"You know, when I came to this place, the whole entrance was full of garbage. It took me three days to clean everything out. I had four huge garbage bags full on the curb."

"Have you been sleeping here ever since you got homeless?"

"Mostly. I tried the mission further up the road but all the residents were girls hooked on heroin or crack, and they wanted to beat me up. I couldn't take it so I came to be near the church so God would protect me."

"Are you safe here?"

"Does it look safe to you here?" she asks me slightly annoyed. "This is a bad part of Trenton. Don't come here at night. I just keep to myself and stay out of trouble. I don't want to be beaten up nor raped."

"Don't you have anybody to protect you who could sleep here, too?"

"No. At some point there were two guys who slept here but then they wanted something from me, and I didn't want to. I have never been one to sleep around."

"If I gave you one wish, what would that be?"

"I would wish to have my family ok again. I have three daughters. They are all in their 30s."

"Why don't they help you?"

"I would rather not go into that, ok?" she replies with a stern face.

"Sure, no problem. What were some of the happiest moments in your life?"

"When my daughters were born and when I met this man named Peter, whom I was seeing for a couple of years. The happiest moments in my life were when my parents were still alive."

After chitchatting for a bit longer, I give her some money. She shakes my hand. "Great! Now I can buy myself new sneakers."

As I get ready to go, I ask her how she manages to stay warm.

"Well, I could do with an extra blanket. It gets cold here."

"Ok, I will be back."

I know exactly what blanket she is going to get: a light blue woolen blanket with white elephants that I received from my beloved French grandmother who raised me. It still has the smell of her big, old house and my childhood. I put it in a shopping bag, together with half a bottle of red wine, some chocolates, a well-wishing card, and a rosary from St. James of Compostela. I look for some citronella candles, which would give light and heat, but Home Depot informs me the season is over. I pick up some Chinese food.

I rush back because it is getting dark and I don't feel like being there at night. I have taken longer than expected and am afraid she will have left. I park my car, grab the bags, and head toward the church. As I get closer, I see her coming from the other direction. We smile at each other.

"Hey! I have been thinking. You know another thing that makes me happy is to meet people like you," she says. "Put that in your book, too."

I tell her the story behind the rosary and the blanket.

"You know, I love all religious things. Unfortunately, I will have to sleep on your blanket but once I am off the streets I will wash it and cherish it.

"It's a good thing you couldn't find those candles because at night you just want to disappear in a corner and not attract any attention to yourself. You see, I used to be quite pretty before but now I am very tired because I hardly sleep at night. I have to watch out that nobody comes near me."

She gives me several hugs. "Here is my phone number. I want you to call me in a month to six weeks' time, and I will tell you I am off the streets, ok? When I am back on my feet, we will go for coffee, and I will make you a big apple pie. I am great at baking apple pies!"

Natural medicine

Tuesday, 9 November

Francisco, a handsome man from Colombia wearing a white baseball cap and a black leather jacket, is sitting on the windowsill reading a book.

"Many people believe that money is happiness but I think that the road to get to money is happiness. Money is just the dessert, and with it I can help other people, feed the homeless, and pay somebody's medication. If I start looking for money, I will not be happy. If I have empathy for others, treat them with respect, serve them, start looking for a better job: This is the true secret to happiness.

"I used to have it all—a nice house in Staten Island, a car, a good job—but I lived all for myself. When I lost everything, I even lost my friends because I had lived only for myself and not for others."

He opens his backpack. "I want to show you something." He takes out a black t-shirt. Written on it in big, white letters is: "What if your main job in life is…?" He lets me think for a moment, then he turns the t-shirt, revealing what is written on the back: "Being happy. A gift you give yourself and others."

We both chuckle for a long time.

"Francisco, tell me three things that make you happy."

"Love. When I find somebody who loves me, and I love, somebody to trust and who trusts me totally because love makes miracles happen and women work with love.

"My job. I work in a metal assembly factory but this week I have a mandatory one-week lay-off. But I really don't mind. I go to Barnes & Noble and read and read and read. I take notes."

He shows me two notebooks with neatly written comments.

"I like to read all kinds of books—*Men Are From Mars, Women From Venus, The Secret, The Power*—but also about the Greeks because this is where our civilization came from. Did you know that they were the ones who started with inflation? They would take gold coins and file away some of the gold and hence, diminish the value of money.

"Natural medicine is another source of happiness. I know quite a lot about it, and it makes me happy to share my knowledge with others and try to help them. I never do it for money. I always tell people there are seven important things in life, in order to conserve a good physical and mental health: the healing power of the sun, your trust in almighty God, the way you think, resting, sleeping, the air you breathe, the type of food you eat, and abstinence from drink and cigarettes. I take an occasional beer but that's about it.

"In Spanish, we have a saying that goes, *'Tu no sirves para vivir, si no sirves a la gente,'* meaning 'Your life is not worth living, unless you are useful for other people.' Why do you think they call the 'Dead Sea' the 'Dead Sea', Elisabeth? It's because it only receives effluence; it doesn't go or give water anywhere."

"How would you end this sentence: 'In order to be happy, you have to…'?"

"In order to be happy, you have to change the way you think, all the wrong thoughts. Don't blame yourself; it doesn't help you. The most important thing is today because today is a gift and today brings the past of the future. I try to purge all old thoughts, read, take notes, and learn new things."

"What was one of the happiest moments in your life?"

"When I fell in love with the woman of my dreams. It was back in Colombia. I had met her once, and we had a little fling. Her name was Leticia, and I couldn't get her out of my mind and kept dreaming about her. I didn't see her for seven years, and then one day I went to church and there she was, dressed in a white dress and coming toward me.

"'I can't believe it's you!' We both exclaimed. Later that night the church had a dinner for the youth. I had been invited there so I went. I started looking out over the restaurant. All of a sudden I saw Leticia coming my way. Next to me there was a spare seat. 'Come and sit down here!' I told her. That was it. We lived together; we broke the rules of the church, which are very sacred in Colombia. She worked for the church and studied theology to be a pastor but they had warned her that she would not be able to get a job as a pastor being a woman. However, there was one member of the church who had money and was quite powerful, who offered her a position as a pastor in a small, rural area. She accepted, and we both moved there. We lived happily like that for a while. One day she was asked to go and give a speech in another village and asked me to come with her. For some reason I did not want to go to that village with her, and she became very upset with me. From there, everything went downhill in a matter of 15 days. Our life together lasted exactly one year." He sighs.

Look your best!
Wednesday, 10 November

"In order to be happy, put yourself first. Always keep yourself looking and feeling beautiful. Take care of yourself, the way you dress, make sure your nails are always well manicured. The hair is definitely very important. Set your best foot forward and try not to have regrets. Take everything life throws at you as a learning experience."

Kisha, hair stylist

Forgive yourself
Friday, 12 November

"Being happy also entails being able to forgive a lot—I am talking about total forgiveness in which you have no rancor in your heart. You also have to be able to forgive yourself."

Ana, law student from Dominican Republic

Being born a sunflower
Sunday, 14 November

Ginnie waves excitedly as she crosses her lawn toward me. Her white hair is short, almost boyish, her figure slim, and her gait light. She wears blue jeans, a turquoise turtleneck, matching turquoise earrings, and a long necklace of colorful beads—the sort that children would make.

I met Ginnie four weeks ago while attending a meeting in the borough hall of Roosevelt Township, where longtime residents were speaking about their lives. She was the first speaker of the night: Her personality and storytelling mesmerized me. At the end of that evening, I asked to interview her. "Of course," she had replied, "Here is my phone number. Call me and you can come over for tea." And here I was! In front of her two-story white cinderblock, bauhaus-style home.

"Be careful when you walk around in the house because we have different levels here. Let me take you on a tour," she says as we enter.

Most walls have white wooden paneling, and the floors are of light wood. A sofa in the entry is vintage 1960s with five colorful cushions neatly lined up next to each other. Along one of the walls stands a beautifully crafted table with round shapes. "My second husband did it," Ginnie tells me. It is gorgeous. A desk stands against another wall. "My first husband made it," she says when I admire it. There are so many tables and chests made by either husband number one or husband number two that it's hard for me to keep track of who made what.

The kitchen extends into a dining room surrounded by large windows overlooking the garden and tall trees.

We proceed to the sunroom, where encased bookshelves line the walls. A flat-screen television, which I suspect isn't frequently used, sits on a table. Seeing me notice it, Ginnie confirms my thought.

"I think that television was the first thing that separated us. Before we all used to listen to the radio together; and then when some of us first got television, we would all sit and watch it as a group. There would even be people standing outside looking through the windows. But nowadays people watch television alone."

Dismissing the television, she moves on with her tour. "This is Markus. He is 35 years old," she says, pointing to a brown and yellow turtle at the bottom of a large glass box, who is taking cautious steps on small wooden chips. Two lamps with bright lights shine straight down on him. "Usually, I let him crawl around on the floor but he is getting tired. Soon he will hibernate for three months. He just sleeps and doesn't eat anything. I am not sure if he even drinks, and I never see him pooh."

After watching him for a while, we go back to the dining room where books and copies of *The New Yorker* magazine are stacked on one end of the oval table. The chair at the end of the table has a small cushion so Ginnie can sit higher. Tapestries, porcelain plates, and paintings decorate the wall. It is such a wonderful house and exudes peace and warmth!

"Would you like some tea, Elisabeth?" Ginnie asks as she waves two different teabags.

Some delicious orange and chocolate cookies as well as assorted nuts serve as snacks.

Before I even can come up with a question, Ginnie starts talking.

"I truly believe that happiness is luck. I have friends who have a very limited capacity for happiness. If you are born with an open temperament and a keen sense of humor, you have an advantage that will never leave you. You don't deserve credit for it.

"For five consecutive summers, my daughter Alison and I would go backpacking for one month. She and I vowed a long time ago never to let a man get between us. We were never as free as when we travelled together. We never had a lot of money but once we had paid for the airfare, we knew that we were safe. We went to many places: England, Scotland, France, Serbia, and Macedonia. One summer while in Spain I remember seeing fields of sunflowers: They follow the sun and the light. I compare them to temperaments because they follow the light. With happy people, it is the same: They follow anything good, any possibility for laughter and for fun. But again, sunflowers are just lucky: They were born sunflowers. I was a sunflower kid. I went from lap to lap between my grandmother, my aunt, and my mother."

I love listening to her. There is so much energy, so much vibrancy in her being.

"Ginnie, what is your definition of happiness?"

"I would have to quote Darwin. Happiness is accepting the Darwinian premise that there is a joy, a fantastic joy, in the 'brief privilege of consciousness.' I think that if I had a mantra, this would be it. If only everybody would be lucky enough to see life that way: the brief privilege of consciousness! Anyone who dies before their time is not given a long privilege of consciousness.

"Just being alive is a privilege! Problems are part of the package, and that's some package because dead is very dead!

"It's because of this that I am not a good hater: I cannot hate forever. We are all alive at the same time: That's an enormous bond. I don't think hugging hate is good for the hater. My mother was a lesson because she was too envious; it infringed on her ability to be happy.

"We can also change and alter our mood at will—by reading or dancing. A lot of us mistake depression with natural sadness. We don't expect a minute of discomfort. We hate being inconvenienced. We are so spoiled. I watch my friends; they pop pills every day."

"What were some of the happiest moments in your life?"

"Falling in love with my first husband, Mort. At the time I lived with my mother and my grandmother in a one-bedroom railroad flat in northern New Jersey. There was a lot of love and a lot of lima beans!" she laughs.

I try to write as quickly as possible. Once in a while I take a break to look at Ginnie against the backdrop of the fallen orange and red leaves on the ground outside the window. Listening to her is like being in a movie. I am mesmerized and so grateful to be there with her.

"Mort was a courthouse reporter. He was the youngest of a Russian-German immigrant family. He came to this country by boat, and he told me he remembered when he was six years old being lifted up on somebody's shoulders to look at the Statue of Liberty. That was his first Lady! They lived in great poverty in an Eastside tenement. They were five boys, and he slept on the kitchen table.

"I had taken a summer job at the *Hudson Dispatch*; this was my first newspaper job. I was a social reporter and had to interview every couple before they were allowed to place a marriage announcement in the newspaper: I had to ascertain their engagement announcement. I met Mort in the library of the *Hudson Dispatch*. At the time I was 19 years old and lived with my aunt and my grandmother. One evening we had just put the paper to bed, and I had missed the last bus home, so I went back to the City Room of the *Hudson Dispatch*. 'North!' I said to Mort.

'Edwards!' he replied and tamped the tobacco back into his

pipe—this was his characteristic move. He agreed to drive me home. He came out with a double-breasted green herringbone suit with a brown tie. Oh God! Did he have bad taste! The drive only lasted 25 minutes but I had found the person I loved and the person I wanted to have children with. I never stopped loving him. This was supposed to be my last day on the job, and I was to resume my second year of studies at NYU, but as soon as I got home that night I called my boss and told him I would not return to school but wished to continue working for the *Dispatch*.

"Mort was every parent's nightmare: He was eleven years older than me and married to a pretty, wonderful woman named Beth. When I met him they were getting separated. Nobody got hurt in this divorce. It was a win-win situation. Beth fell in love with the inventor of Arid deodorant, and I got Mort. She went off to be rich and happy, and I went off to be poor and happy! Mort was only five feet tall. Every single week he wanted to volunteer for the Army but they told him he was too short, and that they didn't have uniforms his size. He never gave up, though. At the time I was five feet, six inches and wore very high heels. When we started going out, I began wearing sneakers but he wanted me to wear my high heels. 'You could walk in the gutter, and it wouldn't help,' he used to say to me.

"My house in Roosevelt was just paradise. His friends became my friends. Roosevelt was very isolated; there was not much traffic but a lot of good traffic. We visited—we never had dinner—there wasn't enough money for that. All visits took place after supper. We would play charades and affairs. We hitchhiked in and out of town. We had a wonderful doctor, Dr. Cox. His fee depended on what he saw. He would settle for a cup of tea or a hug. When you were in trouble, friends would step in and wonderful things would happen.

"Mort was the best, and all my family got to love him as much as I did."

She pauses for breath and looks through me, lost in her memories. I keep silent and savor her story, which has begun living inside me.

"What were other happy moments in your life, Ginnie?" I say gently.

"I cannot even single out happy moments. On most days there has always been a happy moment, even when you feel sick. Mort was sick the last seven years of his life. He was the world's best patient! It's terrible to know you cannot stop death! We had so much as a family: I was the yeller and the swatter. We always took trips but never on the Turnpike—that was too expensive. He was a fantastic man! Love is funny!

"Mort and I got married three times: The first time was at the Mayor's house with just our best friends. The second time we married Orthodox, in his parent's Eastside tenement apartment building. I wore a short-sleeved dress. When his mother saw this, she snatched a scarf off a bureau to hide my nakedness, and since brides are supposed to have veils, she took a tablecloth and draped it over my head. I did not understand a word: Everything was in Hebrew, German, and Yiddish. We had an awful time, me with the tablecloth and the bureau scarf. And at some point, when I would be given a cup with wine, I was supposed to take the first sip and let him finish it. But I liked to drink and didn't know about this tradition, and whooo! I drank it all. I was sorry it wasn't scotch!"

We both laugh for a good while, then she continues.

"After World War II, Mort's family had lost people in the concentration camps. I thought we should be unified so I converted to reformed Judaism and took all the mandatory courses.

"The rabbi came down to perform the conversion ceremony. Later on that day, after dinner at our house, the rabbi said to us, 'Why don't we just have a marriage ceremony?' I was married to Mort for a third time with a dish towel over my head." She inhales deeply and adds, "I would have married him every day!"

I let her words linger before continuing.

"Ginnie, tell me three things that make you happy."

"I really cannot pick three things. Of course, family and friends are understood. Everything living, from leaves to snakes. I just like being part of it all. Reading and music would be a third thing. Since I live alone, I can lurch around and dance whenever I feel like it. I was alone for ten years between husbands, and it has now been 13 years since my last husband died.

"Ferris, my second husband, was a little gift from Mort's doctor. During the last years of his life, Mort was in the hospital a lot so I got to know his doctor and his wife pretty well. Ferris had his own little plane and would take people for flights. The doctor and his wife had won a short flight with Ferris. After their trip they invited me for dinner to their house with strict instructions 'Wear a skirt!' I wore a skirt obediently.

"At this dinner they had also invited Ferris. When I saw him, I thought, 'Thanks, but no thanks!' I later learnt that he had told the doctor that I was 'too schoolteacherish.'

"We ignored each other for three months, and one day he called me up and said, 'Let's give it another try and go out for dinner.'

"Ferris was a great designer. He would always say, 'Don't eyeball it, measure it!' He had a gruff voice, and all the women in Princeton were after him. He had a plane, and he was tall.

"The first time he invited me to his house for dinner I was the only guest. He served kidneys, of all things! He explained, 'I always serve organs because they heat women up!' After dinner he said, 'Let's go to Princeton and go for a flight!' There was a really tattered plane. I didn't care if I lived or died. I just took care of old people (my mother and my aunt) and attended prayer breakfasts. I crawled up the wing and climbed into the plane. There was just enough room for two people. The name of the plane was '21 Victor.'

"When we were about to take off, he couldn't raise the wheels. He said, 'Take this gum. Chew it fast!' I did as I was told, and after giving it to him, he stuck it down to secure the wheel to stand up. It worked, and we were in the air! We used to fly everywhere."

Ginnie gets up to put on some more water for tea. I look at the back of her garden, where large orange fish swim peacefully in a pond with a waterfall. I could sit here forever.

"Ginnie," I say as she returns with more tea, "if you had one wish, what would that be?"

"I hope I can be a good sport right through the end of my life and not whimper, complain, or fight it. You don't fight age at a certain time. If I could have my aunt and my mom back, guess what I would tell them? I wouldn't tell them I love them and thank them for all the good times that we had. They know that. I would only say, 'You were such good sports!' They were able to take life as it came. What would I tell Mort and Ferris if they were here? 'You were so cheated out of aging, which is a fascination in itself. Thanks for all the stuff you left me.'"

"Are you happy, Ginnie?"

Without hesitation, she answers, "Yes, I really am. I cannot even describe it. I feel high a lot of the time. My son has been trying to get me to smoke pot for 20 years but I don't need anything of that sort."

It has been a long interview, and my head is swimming with details but I need to ask Ginnie one more question.

"Do you have any additional thoughts about happiness?"

She takes a sip of her tea, and I notice she has barely eaten any of the cookies—I have eaten far too many.

"We talk so much about happiness. We are as obsessed with happiness as we are with our health. How can you be happy if you are asking yourself if you are happy or happy enough? The trick is to recognize the happy moment. Oh! I am breathing. We do think so much about ourselves. Just don't hold on to bad stuff. You have to figure it into the equation if it exists.

"It's not good to shut things away. The mind has so many rooms. You have to be able to enter every one of them. You don't have to stay there long but you have to enter every room. If we were able to enter every room, we wouldn't need so much therapy."

Infinity

Monday, 15 November

"You remind me of Che Guevara!"

These were my first words when I met Alejandro, my Colombian friend, on one of his rounds delivering mail to our office a year ago. It was also talking to him that I got the idea of embarking on my happiness quest.

Today we sit in a tranquil corner of my favorite Brazilian restaurant, and I am eagerly waiting to hear his thoughts about happiness.

"Happiness, to me, is my child's laughter. It's a rebirth of myself. I can recreate myself. I no longer need to carry the baggage of my past. With my son, I feel more liberated. His joy is a validation of my rebirth."

He sips his campirinha. "I think happiness is also finding happiness in human contact, physical and emotional." He searches for my hands over the table. His hands are soft and warm. "We are all energy—energy is conducted through the hands. By the sense of a touch, you can feel whether a person is happy or not."

I look at him through the flickering lights of the candles: slightly long hair, a hint of a beard, and two studs decorate his ears. He wears a striped red, blue, and green tie under his navy-blue woolen sweater.

"I love anything that revolves around the notion of infinity. For me, happiness is too small of a word to encapsulate the bliss and abundance of infinity. When I look at the sky, and truly break it down—the stars, the dark, the light, the planets, the vast emptiness—it puts things into perspective in life. I realize how precious and yet how insignificant I really am. I feel connected to everybody and everything because we are all in that infiniteness.

"When I look at the sky, I feel that I am not alone. It brings me peace, and it affirms my very deep belief that life is what we make of it. Our life world view is as broad or narrow as we make it. I feel fortunate to take my thoughts away from the limited thoughts and on to the expansive and never-ending.

"Another thing that makes me happy is when I see family, close friends, and acquaintances smile with their eyes. To see wrinkles in the sides of the eyes is the sign that things are going the right way. I like to see things that go down, go up, and things that go up, go down because without one or the other, you cannot understand the other."

Alejandro leans back in his chair and runs a hand through his hair.

"I like the breath and the scent of a woman, all their scents—their armpit, their breasts, their vagina, their hair—because the smell is a sense that we mostly take for granted for those of us who can see. The smell represents who they really are. Some taste bitter like coffee, while others taste like roses."

I let his words sink in for a while before proceeding.

"How would you end this sentence: 'In order to be happy, you have to...'?"

"I would say that for me, in order to be happy, I have to look at myself in the mirror with my soul, and my eyes closed. It implies to truly envision who I am. We are happier if we are being honest at how we look at ourselves; we will find the truth and the lies in the image. This image can be changed by our own inspiration and our ability to see ourselves for whom we really are: for better or for worse. I have to accept myself and make change where I think change is due.

"The biggest pain is when we are on our deathbed and we have to introspectively look at ourselves, our lives, the lives we lived, and we ask ourselves the question: 'Did I live a true moral and ethical life according to my values?' And if the answer is 'no,' are we ready for those implications and the weight that this carries on our final hour for our eternal spirit?

"Similarly, if the answer is 'yes,' are we open for the endless possibilities that are about to occur?"

He removes his glasses. "You know what I think? That we are spiritual beings having human experiences, not human beings having spiritual experiences. It makes more sense. We live in an infinite universe. We are infinite beings with infinite potential and infinite dreams. We are infinite happy gods; we just don't realize it!"

Happiness is eating ice cream
Wednesday, 17 November

My dog, Chino, and I are heading for the playground in search of a person to interview. Two little boys wearing blue jeans and bottle-green sweatshirts are brandishing their baseball bats and playing hide and seek.

"Hi guys!" I ask, "Are your parents around?"

"Yes, they are over there." They point to a burgundy minivan.

I walk to their car, introduce myself, and ask if I can interview their children. They look at each other, nod, and their dad accompanies me to the playground.

Jonathan and Kevin, identical twins, seven years of age, do "rock, paper, scissors" to determine who goes first. Jonathan sits down next to me on the bench while wiggling his feet.

"Tell me three things that make you happy."

"That the trees change colors, that the ocean is blue, and cats."

"Do you have a cat?" I ask him.

"No, but both of my sisters have some kind of hamsters. They are really cute."

"If you had to say, 'Happiness is…,' what would you say?"

Jonathan looks at me with big eyes, then to his dad but remains silent.

"It's kind of difficult. I am going to give up soon."

"Never give up," I reply.

He tilts his head, looks up and down, left to right. "Ok, I give up."

The dad intervenes, "What's happiness to you, Buddie?"

"Happiness is eating ice cream!" He smiles broadly.

Kevin runs to and fro playing with his baseball stick distracting his brother.

I thank Jonathan, and he runs off to the slides. It is now Kevin's turn.

"Kevin, what is happiness to you?"

"Happiness to me is a happy face, when I see somebody who is happy. Happiness is also Chuck E. Cheese's, a place for kids with lots of arcades, toys, and where they serve pizzas, hamburgers, and hotdogs."

"Tell me about some of the happiest moments in your life?"

"Every time I play with Jonathan, when I shoot hoops with my dad, play baseball with a real baseball bat, and my mom's birthday because we eat a lot of cake."

His reply regarding his mother's birthday puzzles me so I ask his dad.

"Well, I am the romantic person in this marriage so we try to spoil Mom. I also want to teach the boys that they have to take care of their mom and their future wives."

Life is short, enjoy it
Thursday, 18 November

"Life is short so why not enjoy it in happiness?"

Fabiola, customer at Barnes & Noble

Being among Cossacks
Sunday, 21 November

"Anatoli!" I exclaim.

A stocky, middle-aged man with a long, white mustache reaching below his chin and wearing a black leather coat and black pants walks toward me. We shake hands. He has big, rough hands.

Anatoli is the president of the New Kuban Education Welfare Association and the Free Cossacks Cultural Center in New Kuban, a township in New Jersey initially formed in 1953 by Cossacks who fled from Russian persecution.

As I step inside the Center, a vast hall opens up in front of me. Large paintings of Cossack battles, heroes, and landscapes adorn the walls, tables covered with burgundy plastic tablecloths sit in the middle of the room, and a ping-pong table and a huge stereo system stand toward the end of the hall under a large stage.

Anatoli proudly shows me the first Cossack flag dating from 1920 with the seven coats of arm of the Cossack tribes. In 1920 Cossackia had been declared an independent country but it only lasted for a few months. Next to the flag is a *"bunchuk,"* which was the 18th century battle flag of the Zaporozhian Cossacks.

"Are you ready for the museum, Elisabeth?"

I follow him through a door that opens onto the courtyard, where two sturdy chickens are strolling leisurely. A few feet away we enter another door that leads us to the museum. It is a large room containing rows of books, publications, coins, costumes, sabers, daggers, pistols, sculptures, belts, and other Cossack memorabilia. Anatoli has gathered most of it through the internet but also through gifts and donations.

"We started building this center in 1969. Cossacks from all over the world would send money. Others would send books. We have recorded everything here. But there was seldom a lot of money, and it was only in 1983 that it got a roof. At that time there was no heating or electricity here. As you can see, it's still not completed. We are also finishing a large sauna, enough for 16 people.

"Any day now we are expecting a silver and jewel encrusted *'bulova'*—a national treasure that belonged to a scepter—that was used at the declaration of the 'Cossack National Freedom Movement' in 1927. It's on its way from Australia."

In the middle of the room hangs a beautiful burgundy robe that had been used by a priest during "*Pokrova*" (a Cossack holiday that has been followed since 1634, when the Virgin Mary came to the assistance of the Cossacks in a battle at Azov).

Anatoli continues, "After the Tsar abdicated in 1917, he felt he no longer needed an army so he decided to dismantle his special convoy, largely made up from Kuban and Terek Cossacks. But from 1918 to 1921, the Red Army chased the Cossack army all the way to Crimea. In 1921 the Cossack army was pressed against the frozen shores of the Black Sea. What would happen if the ice was not strong enough to support the weight of 20,000 men? Before embarking on this perilous journey, the Chaplain held a service for all his men while wearing this red cape, then they got on their horses and went on the ice. The ice held miraculously, and the Cossack army was able to escape along the shore all the way to Greece.

"Elisabeth, look here!" He points at two names in a thick book.

"This is the name of my father's father. He was a Centurion in the Tsar's Convoy. The Tsar would have a Special Convoy of 1,280 soldiers all made up of Kuban and Terek Cossacks. My grandfather was in charge of 100 men." A few lines below this one he points to another name. "This is my wife's grandfather. They served in the same convoy. I have always wondered if they knew each other."

His face becomes somber. "After the fall of the Tsar, my wife's father was forced to see his own father executed by the Red Army in their own yard. The Red Army would chop them up as cabbage."

We both remain silent.

"Are you ready for some mead?" he asks me.

I look at him questioningly.

"We make our own mead here: It is wine made out of honey."

We return to the great hall. I sit down at a table, and Anatoli returns with a plastic cup with dark, sweet mead. It is now time for the interview.

"I am happy when I can get up in the morning and not be in a lot of pain. You see, through the years I have had so many injuries, and this has given me a lot of pain. A few years ago I had a quadruple bypass; I have six compressed vertebra and a torn-out shoulder. But this is the life of a Cossack. Never give up!" he laughs. "I am happy to be in the company of my people. The other night three friends came around, and we were digging up trees for transplantation. The sheep and the cows were running around, and the guys were so happy to see this because it reminded them of home. After working, we had some drinks together."

He takes another sip of mead and wipes his large mustache. "My wife is pretty sick, and I am happy that she will be able to get an operation in two weeks' time. You see, even in sickness you can be happy for small things. It's in the Lord's hands: If you believe in Him, you don't have to be afraid."

"Anatoli, what is your definition of happiness?"

"It's to live like a free human being."

"If you had one wish, what would that be?"

"I wish I would never hear the word 'Russia' again."

"What were some of the happiest moments in your life?"

He looks down at his hands for a moment.

"I think one of the happiest times in my life was when I met General Getmanov (a Kuban Cossack who lost an arm while fighting for the Tsar against the Germans in World War I but who still fought against the Reds in the Russian Revolution as well as in World War II; he later emigrated to Serbia and then to the U.S.). When I was 22 years old, I came to New Kuban, and I helped him to fix his well. He had a small property with a tiny little house. When we became friends, he was in his 80s (he was born in 1890). He started telling me stories about Cossacks that I had already heard 15 years earlier. 'Stop telling me fairy tales!' I said to him. I was perplexed and told him that as a child, my grandpa had sent me to the village that served under him to learn about my history. But at the time I was not told that it was the truth (it would have been too dangerous). So when I met Getmanov, it hit me really hard. This was truly the history of our people! He then told me that he had known my grandfather. They had fought together in World War I. When he settled in New Kuban together with other Cossacks, they had lived like back home: They had their own church, picked wild mushrooms and berries, made wine out of anything you could imagine, and had a few animals (pigs, cows, and sheep). Shortly after we became friends, he got very sick and died but meeting him really brought me back to my reality, to who I was."

He stops talking. I let the silence linger and admire the paintings depicting Cossack scenery.

"I have 13 sheep, six cows, and 22 pigs on my property, which is anywhere between four and a half to five acres," he continues. "The pigs roam so freely that sometimes they come to visit us here. I live the way I used to live back home. I was 12 years old when my parents and I settled in Pennsylvania but I still remember what home was like."

"Tell me about two other moments that made you really happy."

"I guess it was when my youngest son was born. He had more heart but I really think it was because he was a true Cossack. He is 25 years old now.

"A third happy moment in my life was when I was elected permanent '*ataman*.' An '*ataman*' is an elected chief of a Cossack village."

"Anatoli, are you happy?"

"I guess I am as happy as I can be. I am not a person who jumps for joy. I had two very close calls this last year. It didn't really impress me. When I lived in Russia, people were disappearing left and right. When I was five years old my friends would tell me, 'They took my daddy away.' We would never see him again. The secret police used to kill off thousands."

"What is your definition of happiness?"

He reflects for a while. "I think that happiness is what you make it. The contractor I used to work for was a cheapo who never gave me enough material, and I was nervous and disgusted. I could be miserable but instead I would sit here in solitude for an hour, just look at the paintings, and look at this place that we built, and this would make me feel much better."

My Islam

Tuesday, 23 November

The air is crisp and the sun is shining as I walk down Fifth Avenue scouting for a "happiness date." At a street corner I meet Ahmad, who is selling hotdogs, shish kebabs, and roasted chestnuts from a large cart.

"Ahmad, tell me three things that make you happy."

"To serve people. When you are a religious person, you have to serve others, and your God will be satisfied with that. I may not make a lot of money doing this but money will never make people happy. It is just a means to survive. My Islam advises me to be peaceful with everybody. I treat everybody equal, regardless of a person's origin. We have a saying that goes, 'The way you treat people shows how religious you are.' Because our Islam preaches forgiveness, you have to treat people with forgiveness, too. When I satisfy Allah by serving others, He will satisfy me, too.

"When I love my parents and do my best to serve them, I am very happy. I am American and raised in the U.S. but born in Cairo. Here I feel that youth don't have loyalty to those who gave birth to them. How could I deny anything to those who gave me life? In this country many people disrespect their parents."

He is silent for a while and moves the chestnuts on the grill.

"You know what? The third thing that makes me happy is something I didn't do but I wish I would have done it. If I would have done it, I would have been very, very happy. I should have married at 21 years old. Even though I would have made little money, I would have had kids, who would carry my name. Like little plants, I would have seen them grow up. Since I would have gotten them young, they would become like my friends later on in life. We are created to build life. American communities are good communities, and I love it but here many people get children very late: How can you see them grow up and enjoy them?"

He speaks in a passionate manner, and his curly black shoulder-length hair shakes excitedly. Once in a while he sits down on his wooden stool.

"How would you end this sentence: 'In order to be happy, you have to...'?"

"In order to be happy, you have to be close to your God, which for me is Allah. He will put you on your right path."

An older lady bundled up in scarves and layers of coats suddenly appears and starts chatting with Ahmad. They seem to be old acquaintances. He gives her a hotdog, and she takes a soda.

"I will pay you later!" she says and disappears.

"She is homeless," he explains. I volunteer to pay for her but he refuses. I do not want to insist because I know that in Islam charity is very important. I am sure that Ahmad does his fair share of that.

"If you had one wish, what would that be, Ahmad?"

"I would wish that all the people in the whole world would carefully read the translation of the Qur'an in order to know what real Islam is and forget about all its stereotypes. I want to be a messenger for my people: Islam is not a murderous religion."

"What were some of the happiest moments in your life?"

"The happiest moment in my life was when I went to Mecca two years ago. I felt like I was in the sky or something. You see, going to Mecca is one of five things that Islam is based upon but only if you can afford it and if you are in good health. The other four things are you have to say the Shahadah (which justifies that the only God is Allah and that Mohamed is his prophet), praying, giving charity ("*zakat*"), and fasting during the holy month of Ramadan.

"Every year when we celebrate *Eid*, I get this happiness in my heart. In Islam we celebrate two *Eids*: the first one is *Eid Al Fitr*, when we break our 30-day fast, get together, pray, and eat. The second *Eid* is *Al Adha,* when we slaughter a lamb in remembrance of what the prophet Abraham did. Do you remember how Allah had ordered him to slaughter Ishmael, his only son, as a test for his love for God? And how when he was about to slaughter Ishmael Allah saved him by replacing a sheep sent from Heaven? Muslims have been ordered to do the same as Abraham did. So when we slaughter a sheep, we please Allah, and that makes me happy because I will be rewarded when I go to Him."

Egypt
Wednesday, 24 November

The bookstore is full of customers but as I notice an older lady with short grey hair, a red woolen sweater, and an intriguing golden pendant, I immediately know whom to ask. Her name is Marcia. A cane hangs on the back of her chair.

"Travelling makes me happy. I have had four replacements over the last years—two knees and two hips—and now I can finally start travelling again. I love to see ancient things, especially in Egypt. I have been on the Nile, seen pyramids, temples, and the Valley of the King." She shows me her pendant, which represents an obelisk with engraved hieroglyphs.

"Why do you have this particular passion for Egypt?"

"I am going to tell you something." She lowers her voice as I lean over the table. "I am Jewish, and as a child, my parents and I lived next door to my grandparents. My father was a well-known rabbi back in Europe, and my grandfather wanted one of his grandchildren to learn Hebrew so I was sent to a Jewish after-school. I remember getting this picture book, a child's illustration of the Bible written like a comic book. That got me hooked on Egypt. I read it from cover to cover. Later my mom took me to the Egyptian pavilion at the Metropolitan Museum of Art, and I have been smitten ever since." She smiles.

"Are you happy, Marcia?"

She becomes pensive, and her face turns serious. "How funny that you would ask me this today! I was thinking about that this morning. I said to myself, 'I have no one to take care of. I can be my own person now.' It may sound selfish but, as an only child, the day I retired I had to become the caregiver, first for my mother and later for my father. My mother had dementia, and my father died two years ago at the age of 95. He would shop and clean until he was in his 90s."

"If this was your last day on earth, what would you do?"

"I would do exactly the same thing I am doing now. Walk, read, and be in New York. All my teacher friends moved to Florida but not me. I love New York. I enjoy talking to people. It's very strange that you would come up to speak to me today, because when I was younger, people that would sit next to me, would just start talking to me…and I loved it!"

Golf

Friday, 26 November

Today's "happiness date" is Newton, a colleague from Zimbabwe who on most days wears a navy or black beret.

"Golf gives me a pleasure that I cannot derive from anything else. I am in a zone with no noise, free from everything that is happening to me. I usually love my phone but when I play I put it on silence. I focus totally on the game. As I walk there, I contemplate how I can get the ball in the next hole. It's the only time I have for myself. I am in competition with myself. I have been beating myself many times, but yesterday I did not do well. I blame it on the weather: When it's cold, you cannot stretch your muscles.

"Helping people—I don't go around looking for people to help but when I find somebody who needs help and what I give makes a difference in their lives—that makes me very happy."

"Could you give me an example of this?"

"Well, for three months I have been paying the salary of one of the teachers from my primary school back home. You see, we lived in a small village where my parents had a small farm with sheep and cows. In first and second grade, the classes were held under a large tree, and when we attended third and fourth grade, the two grades shared a classroom together. I grew up quite poor and did not own a pair of shoes until I was sent away to boarding school in the bush when I was going into seventh grade. This primary school still exists, and it is there where I pay the salary for one of its teachers.

"Talking to people and sharing ideas also make me happy. Since I have come to the UN, I have learnt a lot about people's countries without visiting. Take my office, for instance. We are four people here. I am from Zimbabwe, there is a lady from Ghana, one from the U.S., and a gentleman from Togo. We learn about each other, try to unpack the reasons as to why we do things differently, why we take different routes to a solution. The unfortunate thing is that we die: We accumulate knowledge and experience, then we die with it. That's the most regrettable part. Death is the worst thing in our life: It robs us for everything. I lost my father three years ago and my brother last year: All their knowledge is gone!"

"Newton, what is your definition of happiness?"

"For me to really be happy is to be at peace with myself. It's when you have full clarity of your life, and you don't see or feel any conflicts anywhere within you. To be at peace means to be in harmony: Everything is chiming, and when it chimes, you smile."

"What a beautiful definition! What were some of the happiest moments in your life?"

"When I became a father: I was 32 years old and had the full comprehension of what it meant.

"When I scored an eagle. The last eagle that I got was about 300 yards from the tee-box. I hit with a club called the driver; I was about 30 to 40 yards from the hole, and it went in. It was a Saturday around 2 p.m. It was the ninth hole. Golf is a round of 18 holes, and on that day I had six pars (four shots from one hole to another), one birdie (three shots between two holes), one eagle (only two shots in between), and there were some bogeys. There are people who can play golf for 40 years and not get an eagle. The other eagle I hit from 220 yards, and we just couldn't believe it. We went looking for the ball everywhere, and in the end it turned out that it was in the hole. It was a big feat!"

December

Love

Wednesday, 1 December

"In order to be happy, you have to give and receive love. If you don't have that, it's like you live alone, and nobody can live alone."

Marco, Brazilian tourist in New York

The first time I earned money
Friday, 3 December

It is late afternoon as I circle the café at the bookstore. An Indian gentleman, despite focusing on a large textbook, gives off an aura of friendliness.

"Excuse me, sir. May I ask you a question?"

He looks up, surprised. "I could do with a break right now," he replies. His name is Nilesh, and he is studying for an upcoming certification exam.

"Being in a place like this makes me happy. I have been coming to Barnes & Noble for ten years, just to read, observe people, and have a cup of coffee. I remember when I was not married I would come here alone—my whole family was in India—and I loved being surrounded by books. I found it comforting, and it helped me cope with the absence of my family. It also reminded me of home, where I grew up with lots of books."

He pauses. "One of the milestones in my life was when I ran my first mile without stopping. I am flatfooted, and in India you cannot join the army because you cannot run long distances. I felt it had limited my life. Before I would run a couple of minutes and became so tired. But after reading *Confessions of an All-Night Runner*, I got really motivated. The day I ran my first mile was amazing; it felt unbelievable.

"Another very happy moment in my life was the very first time I earned money. I came to this country when I was 18 years old. In India there is no such concept as working and going to school at the same time in a middle-class family. My first job in the U.S. was for a wholesale store that sold perfumes, where I loaded and unloaded boxes, did sales, and made deliveries. I was very homesick. The first money I ever earned was $150 in cash. I remember buying some blank cassettes that I sent home so that my friends could make copies of heavy metal music that we used to listen to."

Nature

Saturday, 4 December

The miles go by quickly as I speed on the highway while humming to some of my favorite songs, leaving behind a blue sky and entering a realm of wintery grey atmosphere. My goal is the Rankokus Indian Reservation of the Powhatan Lenape Nation Indians in Westampton, New Jersey.

After following a sign for the Rancocas Nature Reserve, I end up in front of a closed gate. Slightly puzzled, I continue farther and arrive at a Nature Center in the middle of the forest.

A sign on the entrance door says: "Open." I slowly push the handle. A gentleman with dark blond hair, wearing olive-colored hunting pants and a navy-blue fleece jacket, is sitting behind a desk, slightly slumped forward.

"Excuse me, I am looking for the Indian Reservation but I don't seem to be able to find it?'

"No, unfortunately, it doesn't exist anymore. It's a shame because they used to organize really nice events," Jonathan, the Audubon representative, replies.

I decide to check out the Nature Center. A beautiful deer skin hangs over a chair, and different types of owls, hawks, and skunks are on display on tall shelves. A black rat snake, a young box turtle, an African clawed frog, a redbelly turtle, and a musk turtle rest in large, clean, well-lit tanks. When I return to the main office, I tell Jonathan about my project.

"I find this idea great. These days the media focuses too much on sad things," he says as he leans back in his chair, pushes away some strands of blond hair from his face, and starts sharing his thoughts.

"The first thing that makes me happy is family. I am an extremely family-oriented person."

"Do you have kids?"

"No, I was never married nor do I have kids. My father passed away about 20 years ago, and my mother earlier this year, but I have two sisters and am very close to my extended family. I have lots of cousins. When I was a young boy my mother, aunts, uncles, and grandmother would rent a large farmhouse in Vermont, and all the cousins would be together. I used to spend two months there. It was wonderful. When I go there now, I hear voices from the past. I feel pangs of sadness but with them a lot of happy feelings also come back," he says dreamily.

"The natural world is another thing that makes me happy. I live in the house where I grew up, and we have a 15-acre lot. I love to see my dog run around in the woods. His name is Angus. He is a three-year-old Belgian Sheepdog who loves to chase deer, rabbits, and squirrels. Just to be among trees makes me happy. They are my favorite beings. They are positive and do nothing negative for us. They give us fuel, oxygen, and building material. When I was younger, I remember reading an article in a newspaper about this gentleman who adapted his polygraph machine to plants and trees: He would place wires on them. He did this study that really impacted me. When he was using Clorox to clean the sink, the algae would send out distress signals to the houseplants who would pick up on it. In another study that he did, he realized that when he started a chain saw the trees would register fright. I think that what makes me the happiest, and for which I am the most grateful, is the natural world.

"I guess the third thing is art. I love all types of art. You see, I am a naturalist and an artist. I love taking pictures, and in my younger years I had a stint at it in New York. But I came back with the tail between my legs." He laughs. "I have now been taking pictures for 31 years as a serious pursuit."

A middle-aged couple walks in to pick up an order of sunflower birdseeds. While listening to Jonathan and his friends chat, I look around the room and notice a stuffed skunk, pheasant, and two ducks. A large selection of books about animals, birds, trees, plants, and parks fill tall shelves. Stuffed animals, toys, backpacks, sweatshirts, and binoculars are for sale. Once the couple leave, I continue my questions.

"What is your definition of happiness?"

"I believe happiness is momentary. It might last a second, a day, or a week but it's fleeting. It's an emotion that also affects you physically. Laughter is part of happiness. My favorite thing in the entire world is laughter, even over sex," he chuckles. "I love those extended spurs of laughter when you can hardly breathe and your stomach hurts. Happiness is also contentment."

Earlier, when talking to the couple, Jonathan had mentioned his disability and how he needed to get a $400 shot every week. I had noticed that he was limping and walking slightly hunched forward.

"Jonathan, earlier you spoke about your disability yet you seem so positive. How do you manage that?'

"I was born with a severe form of arthritis and have suffered periods of depression. Two winters ago I was so depressed that I didn't go out for four weeks."

"Is it okay if I write this down, Jonathan?"

"Sure, I believe that if there were no pain, there would be no happiness either. You see, depression runs in my family. My grandfather and my father suffered from it. What helps me the most is physical exercise; I just forced myself out of it and eventually managed to kick my depression. The doctor wanted to give me medication but I am already taking so many for my arthritis that I didn't feel like taking any more—there are always so many side effects.

"Just last week I celebrated 21 years of sobriety: I used to be an alcoholic and a drug addict from when I was 16 years old until well in my 20s. At that time, when I looked in the mirror, I would see a monster. I would do drugs and drink to make the pain go away. I really think that I had an angel that followed me around. The part that used to worry me was not how much I drank, but how I would get to different places. I would wake up and not remember how I had driven there. I would check my car to see if I had had an accident, if there were any scratches on it. I never got stopped by the police either. I believe the Creator sent an angel to look over me because he wanted me to do what I do now—teach people about His creation: nature.

"I tried to go to a few AA meetings but at that time those who attended were allowed to smoke, and I simply couldn't take cigarette smoke. What made me change was when a woman I loved told me, 'I love you but I will not accept that you are an alcoholic and that you take drugs.' I decided to quit by myself."

"Did you eventually get that lady?"

"No," he laughs, "but she saved my life. What also made me change the course of my destiny was when I adopted the Native American beliefs of the life force being everywhere. Everything is alive."

"Jonathan, how would you end this sentence: 'In order to be happy, you have to…'?"

"In order to be happy, you have to be of an open mind. I am a very broad thinker. Even if I don't agree with something, and you give me material about it, I will read about it. You also have to surround yourself with positive people, and if you can find somebody who can really make you laugh, you should hold on to them."

"What were some of the happiest moments in your life?"

"This particular moment transcends happiness. I was driving down the mountain into the Yosemite Valley. Outside of the natural beauty, there was a spirit I had never felt before. It brought me to tears. It was pure happiness, rapture. You just could feel the spiritual power."

He removes his glasses and places them on the desk.

"Another happy moment was the first time I ever saw a bald eagle. It was 21 years ago, and I had read an article in a magazine saying that bald eagles had been spotted somewhere in the upper Delaware, where the river flows out in New York State, and where you have New Jersey on one side and Pennsylvania on the other. I called a friend, and we both decided to go camping very close to the spot. I was scanning the river with my binoculars. Suddenly, I heard this bird noise and thought it was seagulls. But by looking closer, I saw that they were bald eagles: Two females (they are larger) were sitting in a treetop, and two males were circling while they were pre-courting.

"Another happy moment was when I was fishing with my father on a lake in Vermont. I was probably 16 years old at the time, and we had rented a rowboat: He was really good at it. That day we caught 30 fish. My grandmother thought that was the greatest thing in the world. She was so happy that she prepared fish the next day for breakfast, which I could not understand at the time, of course, but later I did.

"Are you happy?"

"Yes, I am happy, even suffering from depression. I am a positive person, even when life beats me down. I believe in karma."

My mechanical children

Sunday, 5 December

I am nursing a large mug of black coffee, trying to wake up, when Ove, one of my cousins, appears on my Skype screen from Norway wearing a hand-knitted Norwegian woolen sweater and sipping a glass of red wine.

"As you know, cars are my passion so if I see a beautiful car in an exhibit I get a kick from watching it from all angles. I can spend a very long time just admiring one car, how it's built, its shape, curves and lines. Other times, after having read about a car and gathered enough money to buy it, I will be extremely happy when I finally get it home: I will take it for a spin outside Oslo where there are a lot of twisted roads. After checking that nobody is there, I drive the same road very fast and feel slightly on the edge. The car and I become one entity; you give all you got, and nothing holds you back.

"I particularly remember my 24th birthday while I was studying in Glasgow. After saving money for seven years, I purchased my dream car, a British racing green Jaguar E-type. It was a dark, bottle-green color typical on British racing cars. After buying the car, I only had 50 pounds left in my bank account, which was just enough to fill up the tank and drive from London to Glasgow. I did this in record time, sometimes driving as fast as 125 miles per hour. That was a really good feeling." He laughs loudly.

"When I got to Glasgow the Jaguar was in a terrible shape but I had no more money. I tried to sell it but they only wanted to give me half of what I had paid for it so that was not an option. When I met my first wife, she had to fight for my attention because the car was so important to me. Eventually, she grew to love it, too. I kept it for 24 years but a year and a half ago I sold it. The buyer offered me the minimum price that was acceptable to me. But for me, it was important to sell it to a person I liked. When you sell something that has been part of your life for so many years, it's crucial that you sell it to somebody who is as dedicated as I was. And this guy truly was. After he purchased my car, he went for a one-month trip in Europe and drove 3,000 miles."

I can hear the passion in his voice and see the excitement in his eyes as he is talking.

"Twelve or 13 years ago at our summer house I discovered an old toy car. I started doing some research as to what it would cost to buy such a car. At that time it was far too expensive. Since then, I made some money on the stock exchange, and the sorely needed cash became available. Through eBay I found my dream car, an original, flashing red Corvette Stingray Coupe from 1963 with a so-called split window that had not been restored. It was one of the first to be made—actually, it was number 459 out of 11,500 cars that were made—and was completed on 27 September 1962. Its engine has 300 horsepower. I bought it totally unseen from a well-known seller. It was sent home to Norway in a container with three other Corvettes. I was very anxious to see my new car. When I first filled up the gas tank, several liters of fuel ran out of it. Since then, I have had lots of fun with the car. I love its revving engine. To me, it's the most beautiful car ever made, and the Split Window coupe was only produced that single year."

I look out of the window where flurries are falling slowly to the ground.

"Ove, if this was your last day on earth, what would you do?"

"I would make sure that my wife has enough funding to live the rest of her life in a good manner." A wide grin spreads over his face. "If I were single and was given two weeks to live, I would sell my house quickly and buy an Aston Martin V8 from 2015. We planned to rent it some weeks ago when we were in Scotland but it was too expensive. We should have done it," he adds regretfully.

To wake up and see the sun
Tuesday, 7 December

While going for a walk during my lunch hour I meet Troy, an African American man with a small mustache and a tiny beard under the lower lip who is smoking a cigarette while resting on his bike. A tall hat covers his dreadlocks. I notice a blue pen resting behind his right ear.

"Tell me three things that make you happy."

"I love my job. It energizes me, and I look forward to going to work every day. Ten years ago I started my own messenger company. It's only the two of us. My buddy is over there," he adds, pointing at a young man who joins us.

"Do you bike every day, even when it rains and snows?"

"Yes. Sometimes we will take the subway if we have to go to a totally different part of town but most of the time we bike.

"My five kids make me really happy, and being able to see the sun in the morning. I know that here people don't look at it like that, but back home in Trinidad, they think that when you sleep it's almost like you are dead so when you wake up it's like you are alive again."

He adjusts his messenger bag over his shoulders. He tells me he is 48 years old and that he came to the U.S. when he was 21.

"What were some of the happiest moments in your life?"

"Having my first son when I was 38 years old. You see, I was not present when I got my daughter—she was with her mother in Trinidad—maybe that's why we don't have such a good relationship today—so being present at my son's birth was very special. I was also there for the delivery of the three other children.

"The Fourth of July. We celebrate the independence of the United States; we don't go to work, we relax, go to the beach, have barbeques and fireworks."

He hesitates for a while. "I would like to mention my wedding day as a happy day but the U.S. is not a good place to get married."

"What do you mean by that?"

"In this country nobody says 'sorry,' nobody tries really hard to make things work. It's a society where people are used to getting what they want when they want it. It's hard to keep a marriage together." He falls silent for a while. "Well, I guess I could mention my second wedding as a happy moment in my life but it's overrated. It's supposed to be a very special day, and people are supposed to remember why they got married, made vows to each other about what they loved in each other. Too often people say, 'Why did I ever marry you?' Sometimes the passing of time destroys the memory of the wedding day, which is supposed to be beautiful."

"Are you happy?"

"Yes, I am happy."

"Do you have any final words on happiness?"

He adjusts his hat, strokes his chin, and clears his voice. "Live every day as if it was your last. Have hope that tomorrow will be even better than today and that there is a new horizon waiting to be discovered."

A living lion
Thursday, 9 December

From the upper level of the shopping mall I have a perfect view of the shoppers on the main floor, some of them relaxing in the deep leather couches. A man sits upright and seems to study the passers-by. He will be my "happiness date!" As soon as I start talking to him, he pats the couch. "Sit down here!" He wears hearing aids so I move up closer. He is very friendly and seems thrilled to talk to me.

"My name is Jiwand Singh. In my country 'Jiwand' means 'living' and 'Singh' means 'lion.' You are sitting next to a living lion who doesn't look like a lion."

Before I can ask him any questions, the prospective interviewee turns interviewer. "Elisabeth, how long have you been in this country? Where are you from? Are Norway, Sweden, and Denmark really similar? Are you married? Do you have children? Do you consider yourself a happy person?"

After a while, fearing that the wife or some relative will return and snatch him away from me, I turn the conversation around. "Let's talk about you now, Jiwand. Tell me three things that make you happy."

"A positive outlook. I did not have such an attitude all the time but I have been developing my personality, passed through lots of experiences, and have come to the conclusion that being positive leads to a state of happiness.

"I am not materialistically so ambitious. I do enjoy some nice things around me, though, such as a nice house, good clothing, and good food. But I think that the key is simplicity. Simple living and simple thinking because our genuine needs are really simple and few. We don't need a lavish style of life. When I come here to the mall, I like myself more to be known as a spectator than a buyer. I like when good people, such as yourself, come around and smile to me. That's a great thing!"

Jiwand often touches my arm while talking to me and never ceases to smile. It is one of those smiles of a wise man who has learnt the secrets of life.

"God is love! I genuinely believe in the spirit of it! Not that I was all the time loving. I had my jealousy and my narrow-mindedness in early life but I was conscious that was not ultimately to be my way of life. I thank God that I have now grown out of it, and I seem to love all nature, mankind, animals, plant life, and even rocks!"

I enjoy his enthusiasm and honesty. While I am jotting down my notes, I study him. He is wearing grey dress pants, a blue and white striped shirt, a blue sweater, and a cap.

"Guess how old I am?"

I am thinking maybe he is 72 years old but find it better to err on the side of caution.

"68?"

"No," he smiles, "you know the game *The Price Is Right*?"

I nod.

"You go ahead. I will let you know."

And so begins our guessing game.

"69?"

He waves his hands, indicating a higher number.

"70?" More waving.

"71?" He waves again.

I mention every year until I reach...

"90?"

He nods with a broad smile on his face!

"I believe that, genetics apart, your own input has a role in your longevity. As I said, simple living and simple thinking."

"Jiwand, are you happy?"

"I am happy now. I am a contented person and thankful to God that I have everything I need: a good family and three children that I am very proud of. Whatever I wanted, God gave me, even the most unthinkable things." He stops for a while to think. "In the Hindu religion, we have what is called '*vedant.*' It is a philosophy of oneness that comes from the ancient wisdom of the Yogis, which we find in the Indian sacred texts called the '*Vedas.*' There it says that what you see outside is not the real self. The real self is inside. Inside we are all the same: There is no 'you' or 'me.' If I am not able to see Jiwand Singh in Elisabeth, I am not a good Hindu. This is called self-realization. Then there is no difference between the one and the other. When you come to that state of mind, there is no place for hatred because if I hate you, I hate myself."

"What were some of the happiest moments in your life?"

"I was born a Sikh into a Hindu family but the long hair and the turban did not click with me. It was simply not convenient. From the time I was a child, I always had lots of desires: Cutting my hair and removing that turban were two of them. During my early childhood I had felt inhibited and did not feel true to myself. When I was 23 or 24 years old, I decided to cut my hair and remove my head garment—to my parents' great despair—and become what I wanted to be. By cutting the hair and getting rid of the turban, I felt like a prisoner coming out of jail, like a bird fleeing from its cage. I was finally a free man. I was very happy that day and had a wonderful sleep. My parents were not thrilled when I did this but then they ultimately agreed with me because I had not been true to myself. And when they saw how happy I became, it was also easier for them to accept it. I believe that being true to yourself also has to do with happiness.

"In India I retired from a pretty high-level position in general administration. In order to reach that level, there was a very rigorous competition exam: Only 100 out of 25,000 applicants would be selected. Although I never expected to pass the exam, I did. I was 37 years old at the time. I give the credit to God, not to my intelligence. Prior to getting that job, I was teaching mathematics at college.

"As I told you before, when I was a child I had a lot of desires. I wanted to travel and see the world. Up to the time when I cut my hair, I had not yet left my village. I had a strong wanderlust and wanted to see the mountains. Once more my wishes came true, and I was sent for diplomatic service in an Indian aid mission in Nepal. I stayed there for three years and did a lot of walking in the mountains."

He pauses briefly and seems lost to his memories.

"I still want to wander at my age of 90 but sometimes it clashes with my family's schedule. Not that I am not a satisfied person but that lurking desire is still there."

I tell Jiwand about Argentina and its beautiful mountains. He admits that this is a place he always wanted to visit.

"Jiwand, if this was your last day, what would you do?"

"I was afraid to think of it at one time but now I believe that life is a gift from God and that He has given me so much in my life that I will still not be paying my debt if He takes back my life today. That belongs to Him. My life is His life."

Three weeks later I get an excited email from Jiwand.

"My daughter and I are back from Guatemala. We liked the country and the people. Immensely. I did not know that there was more of Mayan civilization in Guatemala than in Mexico. Both the forest and the archaeology were a thrill. All other places where we stayed were scenic, too, overlooking some lake or other, at altitudes of 5,000 to 6,000 feet. The weather remained good. We thoroughly enjoyed the tour."

I was utterly happy to see that my living lion was still travelling and exploring those mountains that he loved so much.

Happiness is from the spirit
Saturday, 11 December

"You ask me about my definition for the word 'happiness.' Hmm! I have a hard time with this word because it seems to be related to something that happens to you, like 'happenstance' (for instance, you are happy because you got money or you saw a beautiful flower today). I prefer the word 'joy' because it is not contingent on something happening, on circumstances. It's something inside of you.

"I think real happiness is something that comes from the spirit. It's difficult to attain but I truly believe in the evolution of man: If you really want something, you will get it. If what you want is good, not only for you but also for others, it will come your way. Like Teilhard de Chardin said: 'Everything that rises must converge.'"

Dan, employee at bookstore

Be in balance
Sunday, 12 December

"In order to be happy, you have to be in balance with yourself and others. You have to pay attention to other people's lives and interests and care for them—all while tending to your own needs as well. You have to live a life in which you don't exaggerate in anything. *Carpe diem*. Seize the moment. Use all your possibilities and opportunities."

Fredrik, Norwegian cousin

Small things that remind you of your humanity
Monday, 13 December

Today's "happiness date" is a Chinese colleague, a delightful young man of 28 years old who has short brown hair and a tanned complexion.

"Tell me three things that make you happy."

"Money."

I am surprised. Very few people come up with this answer. "Why?"

"Firstly, because of all the wonderful things it can bring you. I have very little ambition and have not yet figured out what I want in life. When one doesn't know what to pursue, the next thing after that is money. Money is like the default, a scorecard, an easy target. It's a blessing to know what you want in life but very few people really know it.

"The second thing that makes me happy is sex. It's an affirmation of yourself. I don't want to sound so hippie but it's something so genuine and natural. It's the elephant in the room.

"And lastly, small things that remind you of your humanity, that you are still able to hear the murmur of your consciousness, the whisper of your heart, God talking to you. The feeling of a sunny afternoon. A smell or a light that reminds you of things from your childhood."

"What is your definition of happiness?"

"It's five to ten million dollars, give or take a few millions."

He truly is serious about this money business!

"Are you happy?"

"No. I am about $4,999,999.00 away from being happy."

"What would it take for you to be happy?"

"Well, getting that amount of money, or finding a girlfriend. Maybe if I got either one or the other I would be happy, or maybe if I got both."

We chuckle.

"What were some of the happiest moments in your life?"

"When I saw a girl with pink socks in the subway. In New York everybody wears either black or white. One day I saw this lady in a dark suit but what really touched me were her pink socks.

"When a female salesperson sold me a slim-fit shirt, I was really happy because I am neither slim nor fat. I am happy she saw me in that type of shirt.

"The other day I went down in the street to buy some fruits. I asked the salesperson for the price of the plums. He told me he sold them two for one dollar, then I asked for the bananas, and he replied three for a dollar. I decided to go for the bananas but he still gave me a plum for free. Small acts of kindness make me very happy."

"What is the best memory of your childhood?"

"I come from a small fishing village, located at the estuary where the Yangtze River enters the sea. The Yangtze River was crossing our village. In summer and winter people would go fishing, and in spring and autumn they would farm rice and rapeseeds. I left China when I was 13 years old but there is one memory that stands out: When we opened the windows in the morning, there was the smell of the sun. The villagers would wash their sheets and comforters in the morning and hang them outside to dry so when I opened those windows I remember the smell of the sun in those clean sheets blowing in the wind."

Cooking for my friends

Friday, 17 December

My friend Jean-Michel and I are having lunch in a French restaurant. He is tall, blond, full of energy, and speaks with a heavy French accent. When we finish eating, it is interview time.

"I love to be with my friends, go out with them, but especially cook for them. It's the entire process that I enjoy. Around 7 or 8 a.m. in the morning I go to the supermarket to find the best ingredients. Nobody is there, and I can pick what I want in peace and quiet. This is where my happiness begins. I return home, prepare the meal, and set a beautiful table with nice silverware, flowers, and candles. I then enjoy the cooking and finally, the arrival of our friends and sharing the meal with them.

"Lola, our three-year-old Schnauzer, is one of those things that makes me really happy. She always wants to be petted. It's very relaxing. It's pure love. We have a lot of complicity, and we get each other. She is an amazing dog!" he chuckles, "not just because she is my dog."

The waitress arrives with two flans au caramel.

"Are you happy?"

"I am generally a happy person, get quickly over things, and don't keep negative stuff inside. When I go to bed at night and pull the comforter over me, I put the bad day behind me, and that's it. When I repeated classes as a kid, I learned how to deal with big issues—these are big issues for a child—and this helped me to be able to digest problems growing up."

"What were some of the happiest moments in your life?"

"Until now the happiest day of my life was when I married Raul because its preparation took so much work; we had so many logistical difficulties plus the fact that my mother got breast cancer six months prior to the wedding, and we still managed to get through everything. We only invited people we really loved and cared for. It ended up being perfect.

"Another happy moment was this week when I learned that my mother's test results were fine and that she was cancer free." He smiles and appears slightly hesitant but at the same time bursting of eagerness to tell me something.

I wait patiently.

"What I am about to tell you don't mention it to anyone. You are the first one that will know. Two days ago we got a phone call from the agency saying that they had matched us with a surrogate mother. This is the real beginning of the adventure of being parents for us. We can't wait to meet with her in January. Now we just have to find an egg donor."

Put the happy mood forward!
Saturday, 18 December

There is no way I can write this book without including Dalia, my Egyptian friend, or as I like to call her, "My Dancing Angel."

I was fortunate to be her administrative assistant when she started working for the United Nations. She was of medium height, slender, with lots of unruly, curly black hair that reached just above her shoulders, very often tucked in a beret. My favorite was the red one. She brought light and joy wherever she went. Sometimes I would cross her in the corridors, and she would be singing. She later confessed that she thought the United Nations needed some light tunes to be sung within its walls. She has since moved to Egypt.

And here we are on Skype, she in Cairo, and I in New Jersey.

"Dalia, tell me what makes you happy."

"I am usually happy being with children, especially young children. It's a sure way to change my mood if I am not in a happy place. Since I don't have many children in my life, when I lived in New York I would go to a nearby playground and watch kids play. Their play and interactions would remind me what life is all about, just to play, enjoy life, not to worry, and to have joy.

"Plants and flowers raise my energy in palpable ways. In Cairo every spring we have an exhibit of plants and flowers, which lasts about two months. When I feel a little bit unwell, I go to watch these plants and flowers, and my mood improves immediately.

"Working with plants and gardening is very healing for me. Yesterday I bought some flowers, and every time I pass in front of them I get so happy. If I cannot work with my own hands on my land or planting, I like to have them in pots at home."

"Tell me about your land, Dalia."

"It's a small lot, maybe the size of an acre, that I acquired when I lived in the U.S., situated 40 kms north of the pyramids near the Cairo-Alexandria desert. I really liked the energy this place emanated: It was a fresh, clean, and pure virgin land. Its soils were sandy but of a nice, warm red color. The air in Cairo is very polluted, and its energy is stagnant. Having a plot of land made the thought of returning to Egypt much easier. We put down a watering system, and I planted 80 trees: olives, figs, lots of mangoes, guavas that are now three meters tall, a couple of apple trees, oranges, tangerines, peaches, and nectarines."

I can hear the excitement in her voice.

"I also have okra, a lot of arugula. I am an arugula addict," she laughs. "There is something special about its fresh greenness! Wherever I travel I always bring back home fresh arugula seeds. When I have spent what seems an eternity in the city, I get this feeling of 'I am arugula deficient. I have to go to my land,' and I get in my car, drive to my plot, and get my necessary dose."

"What do you plan to do with your land?"

"My objective is to be self-sufficient and cover all my needs from my garden. Since my lot is small, I cannot provide anybody on a consistent basis with produce. I want to donate to friends, family, orphanages, and homes for the elderly. As it is not really good for the world that I drive back and forth over there too often, I am planning on building a one-room cabin with a bathroom this spring so that I can sit there and do my translations and not have to return to the city at night."

"Is there a third thing that makes you happy?"

"My creative writing gives me a lot of happiness. Up until a few years ago, I suppressed my creativity to do academic work and finish off my PhD. These last few months I feel that I have acknowledged myself as a creative writer and, allowing that, I feel that more of it comes out. Right next to me an 80-page draft of a novel is sitting on my table. Not too long ago I participated in a ten-day silent retreat of the Vipassana tradition. We were not allowed to speak or to write. However, after four days, I felt a strong urge to write so whatever I saw, whatever scraps of paper I could find, I would write on. I could not stop writing: In five days I had written 80 pages.

"Last year I watched a lot of mediocre plays during a theater festival. I started writing a monologue but ended up writing a play. In my life I have directed 14 plays but never written one so, for me, this was very exciting.

"I particularly remember when I was 25 years old and directed my first play. It was chosen to represent Egypt in a theater festival in Morocco. We performed in a really big theater with 3,000 seats. It was almost full. At the end of the night I was sitting in the light booth and giving the engineers the light cues, and I remember saying to myself, 'I am so lucky: I am 25 years old and have been wanting to direct a play since I was eight, and now I am representing my country in a festival in another country.'"

"Dalia, what is your definition of happiness?"

For a few moments I only hear the soothing noise of a teaspoon turning in a cup of tea. Maybe also noise of some cars in the background? I am not sure.

"That's a hard one," she exclaims. "In my case happiness connects to a visceral feeling, not just a mental feeling. I get a fluttering, tickling sensation in my tummy. A sense of excitement."

"Are you happy, Dalia?"

"These last days I have been blessed with nothing outside to make me happy, just my inner happiness, and I would just count my blessings. In spite of financial problems, health issues, traffic issues, my parents' health, and the madness of life, I am quite happy. I find myself doing little screams of joy for no apparent reason. Just living is so good! This is amazing! Nothing has to happen. I just have to tap into my inner well of joy!"

"I think it is very important that every day, deliberately, you put the happy mood forward."

Seeing people smile
Monday, 20 December

"Ding, ding!"

An African American man wearing a dark blue woolen hat with a shirt that says "Salvation Army" pulled over his clothing is shaking a bell. Next to him the typical, red, kettle-shaped container for donations hangs from a stand. I give some money.

"Thank you, miss!"

He is tall, has a deep voice, short grey beard, and wears glasses.

I start telling him about my project but before I can finish he interrupts me. "My name is Marvin. I would love to get interviewed."

"Great. Tell me three things that make you happy."

"Seeing people smile in the morning: I love that. Eating and laughing make me happy. I like to say 'Good morning' to everybody I meet. In Brooklyn where I live, I always go around greeting everybody so now they call me 'Good Morning.' When they see me, they say, 'Good morning, Good Morning!'"

I am getting ready for my next question when he adds, "Oh yes! I love music. You see those boys over there exiting the building?"

I nod.

"Well, they were just inside and played Christmas music. It was beautiful.

"As a kid, we used to do a lot of singing for Christmas. We would open our gifts, look at them for a few minutes, but then came the best part: going into my mother's room and singing carols. We would sing songs the whole holiday season."

As we are talking a few passers-by donate money in the kettle.

"Hey man! How are you doing?" Marvin waves as they drop by and greet him.

"Marvin, what is your definition of happiness?"

"It is simply waking up and feeling joyful from early in the morning. Happiness makes you feel all giddy."

"What were some of the happiest moments in your life?"

"When my kids were born were definitely the best moments in my life. They are now 34, 30, and 29 years old.

"When I was singing and made the All City Choir. This is one of the biggest choirs there is out here. I sang in that choir for one year. I was the best baritone in all five boroughs.

"Working for the Salvation Army. I have so much fun doing this. Every morning I look forward to going to work. This is my fourth year. We do it for the months of November and December. I love doing this and seeing people smile. Sometimes they tell me they don't have money but then I just answer, 'Doesn't matter. Just give me a smile.' They smile at me, and many times they will come back later in the day and give me some money. Others will bring me a cup of coffee, tea, or hot chocolate when it's really cold."

"If I gave you one wish, what would that be?"

"I wish I could find a nice, happy woman to share my life with."

"Are you happy, Marvin?"

"Yes, I am happy. Oh yeah!"

"How would you end this sentence: 'In order to be happy, you have to…'?"

"In order to be happy, you have to keep an open mind about everything in life, and don't let anybody steal your joy!"

Being with my parents
in their last years
Wednesday, 22 December

It is 6 a.m. My son and I are on an airplane from Newark to San Francisco to catch a connecting flight to visit my husband in Japan. We sit in separate rows so I am expecting a fellow passenger—a potential "happiness date?"—any time. Very soon a tall, blond, nice-looking man wearing a light-green and white checkered shirt and jeans sits down next to me. We strike up a light conversation. His name is Randy, and he has been to Japan 70 times.

"Are you able to sleep on planes?" I ask him.

"In the beginning I wasn't but now I am. You will see!" he replies with a big grin.

I laugh and try to close my eyes to get some rest myself. I ponder: "How will I manage to interview two people in a day, being that I lose one day due to time difference and that I will sit next to my son on the next leg of the trip?"

I turn toward Randy, who is still awake. "I would like to ask you a favor. I have been interviewing one person a day about happiness since 1 January, and so far I have not missed a single day. I know it's really early but would you mind if I interviewed you?"

"Not at all."

I am in heaven!

"Tell me about some of the happiest moments in your life."

He is pensive and far away in his thoughts. "What I am about to tell you is a really odd happy moment because, for me, it was sad but also a happy moment. Both my parents got very ill the last two years of their lives but I was able to spend a couple of years with them. I spent one year with them without working. When you have the opportunity to give back to people who gave you so much, it gives you a lot of happiness. To me, it was a real blessing.

"When you are a child, you have your parents; you look up to them, they are this authoritative figure, you have this parent-child relationship. However, when I spent those last two years with them, I was able to get to know them as real people, friends who were also my parents.

"We spent many hours just talking, and I got to know them very well. I learned about their childhood, their thoughts, their views on things, and how they were feeling. It provided me with an opportunity many people don't get. It allowed me to help them but it also allowed me to find out who I was.

"When they both passed—my mother was 87 and my father 83—within one year of each other, I had no regrets. The fact that I was able to spend so much time with them in the twilight of their lives was a wonderful gift. Even though it was a sad event it was also beautiful, which comes to show that you can have sadness inside happiness."

"Thank you for sharing these moving memories."

"Me watching my father through this, he taught me how to die. He was so at peace when he passed away. He actually helped teach everybody in my family, especially my mother who was so afraid of dying. To me, it was a powerful life experience but with underlying sadness."

"Are you no longer afraid of dying?"

He gives a short laugh. "I went from being terrified with the subject to being able to deal with it."

"How did your dad get ready to die, Randy?"

"Ten years before dying my father found his religion. He even got baptized again. Shortly after that he started writing religious poetry. He wrote many, many volumes of poetry. One year before he died he stopped. I think it was at that time that his preparation for dying ended. He was ready. At the beginning of December of the year he died, the doctor told him that the cancer was at a stage where nothing could be done anymore. He feared that at the age of 83 years old my father's body would no longer tolerate chemotherapy and radiation. My father was asked to think about it, and he decided he would not submit to any further treatment but chose hospice care at home instead. For a while he was doing well. He even drove his car. His last Christmas was wonderful. His brother, whom he didn't see very often, came to visit, and he spoke with many friends and family members that he loved.

"My father had always been a very impatient person throughout all this life but when he found his faith, he learned to be patient. Two days after that Christmas he said, 'That's it. I will no longer eat or drink.' It was like he had seen all those he wanted to see, and he was ready to die. My father had always loved food and used to eat up to eight times a day. Seeing that after a few days of not eating and drinking he was still not dead, and being famished, he declared,

'Okay, I think God wants to teach me one more lesson of knowing the virtue of patience. Besides, he doesn't seem to want to see me yet. I have to be patient.' So he indulged in all his favorite food once more.

"My mother was also ready to die. For the past years she had been on dialysis but toward the end her body did not take to it very well. One day she said, 'This is it. I am ready,' and she decided not to take dialysis anymore; one usually knows that a person will only last for about two weeks. She passed away short of two weeks but she was ready."

Ichigo ichie

Friday, 24 December

This is my first morning in Japan. We have taken the subway to my husband's office. The subways here are incredibly clean; no paper, bottles, or plastic are anywhere to be found, in spite of the fact that following the nerve gas attack in one of the subways in Tokyo in 1995 the authorities eliminated all the garbage cans. Nobody is drinking nor eating on the trains either. Along the walls of each car is one long bench covered in green, royal blue, or brown velvet.

Mayumi, one of my husband's Japanese colleagues, is waiting for me in her office. She has long black hair, glasses, and a wide, red scarf that matches the color of her lipstick.

"To me, happiness is for time to be completely filled with what I am doing. In Japan we have a proverb that goes, '*Ichigo ichie*' ('Each moment has to be lived fully')."

This proverb, which means "one lifetime, one meeting," was first coined by a 16th century tea master in Japan who stressed the importance of each gathering. Since no encounter will come again, each meeting has to be treasured both by the host and by the guest. This is why they always serve each other a light meal and a cup of tea.

"I try to live in the moment. Since the moment never comes back, each moment becomes very precious. When you are aware of this, you can be very happy. I want to keep it as important as possible and to do my best, whether it is eating, working, or talking to you."

Nice classmates

Saturday, 25 December

Before I left the U.S., a Japanese colleague had written down a few words for me, and among them was *"Eigo o hanasemasu ka?"* (Do you speak English?) and, of course, *"Shiawasedesuka?"* (Are you happy?).

I go for a walk after breakfast in search of a "happiness date." It is cold, the wind is strong, and I am relieved I brought my down jacket. People are rushing past me, a lot of them on their bikes. I stop a few pedestrians.

"Eigo o hanasemasu ka?"

Five times, they just shake their head. I mainly target young people, considering that they are more likely to know a foreign language. After walking several blocks, two giggling and chatting young girls turn the corner.

"Eigo o hanasemasu ka?"

"A little bit," one of them replies.

I tell them about my project and ask the one who had answered my question if I can interview her. She accepts. Each question creates hefty discussions between both of them, as they help each other with the vocabulary and come up with answers together. They tilt their heads toward each other and gently tap each other on the shoulder. The person I interview, Mariko, is 16 years old. Her black hair is tied back in a ponytail, and she wears a medium-length, black coat and a short, black skirt with small boots.

"Mariko, tell me three things that make you happy."

"My classmates in high school, my family, and food. I love eating good food."

During my stay in Japan I discover that the latter is a common source of happiness for many Japanese.

"If I gave you one wish, what would that be?"

They both look at me questioningly, and I provide more explanations. They gesticulate, laugh, exchange some words, and cover their mouths.

"I want a good boyfriend." She blushes.

"Ah! What is a good boyfriend?"

They look at each other again, giggle, and exchange more words before answering.

"He should be wise, intelligent, kind, tall, and handsome. Not too handsome, though!"

The wind is blowing some strands of hair in her face. She gently brushes them away. It is quite cold to stand still at the corner of the street but none of us seems to mind.

"Tell me some of the happiest moments in your life."

After another round of glances and conversation, she continues.

"Last year when I was a junior in high school I directed our high school choir, and we won a song contest. We performed pop music. Also when I got many nice classmates in my class this year."

Since she seems at a loss for identifying a third happy moment, and her English is not so good, I stop my questions here. After thanking them, we wish each other Merry Christmas and a Happy New Year. They continue walking tightly huddled together, and I return to my family.

Christmas

Tuesday, 28 December

At 3,776 meters (12,390 feet), Mount Fuji is Japan's tallest mountain. The sacred Mount Fuji or Fuji-san (*san* being a suffix added to indicate gender, either Mr. or Ms./Mrs.) had been glorious. The weather had been perfect. When we stopped at a panoramic viewing site, we were able to see her in all her splendor. A lot of people do pilgrimages to the rim of Mount Fiji but these ascents can only be done in July or August. When you reach the top of the mountain, you look down at an old crater. Women, previously thought to be impure due to their menstrual bleedings, were not allowed up Mount Fuji until 1872.

After lunch we take a cable car from Hakone, a resort city well known for its hot springs, to visit sulfuric steam vents in the mountain. The wind is howling, and the temperature is down to zero degrees Celsius. My son and I decide to brave the elements and walk through a thicket of small lava-resistant bushes, since the trees that previously existed there were destroyed when the volcano erupted, and finally reach the midst of the steam outlets, which have a very strong smell. The hill of the Owaku Dani (Valley of Great Boiling) seems dead and supernatural apart from the steam, which is carried away by ruffles of wind and gives you the impression of being in a cloud of cotton.

In a yellow cabin on this hill, hard-boiled black eggs, resulting from being boiled in sulfuric water, are for sale. Legend says that if you eat one black egg, you will extend your lifespan seven years. If you eat two eggs, you will extend it 14 years. But if you eat three eggs, you will die due to a high level of cholesterol. The advice of our very knowledgeable tour guide Mikki-san was, therefore, to "share the eggs with your friends," since they are sold in packs of five. Shivering in the cold and their hair blowing in all directions, the Japanese tap their eggs against a small table, removing the shell.

On the bus heading back to Tokyo, I approach a young lady who has thick, long, black hair and wears gold and pearl earrings. Her name is Pia, and she is from the Philippines.

"How would you end this sentence: 'In order to be happy, you have to…'?"

"In order to be happy, you have to give more of yourself to

others, and this will give you a lot more in return, even if it's not in this lifetime but in the next one."

"What is one of the happiest moments in your life?"

"Christmas is a big thing for us in the Philippines. We usually celebrate it with a lot of relatives. We invite our extended family and have many reunions. It is also a time to see a lot of friends, new and old. Starting on 16 December and all through 24 December, we attend *"simbang gabi"*—Spanish people call it *"la misa del gallo"*—a church service from 4 to 5 o'clock in the morning. The pastor makes sermons to prepare us for Christ's birth. After the service you eat specialties sold by street vendors outside the church. Once you have completed nine masses, then you are entitled to wish for something. Although it is hard to get up so early, these services really put you into the Christmas spirit. On the 24th of December we go to church before midnight, then we go home where a big feast is waiting for us and open our gifts. During the whole Christmas season, people go caroling. All this makes the Christmas season very special."

To be God's child
Friday, 31 December

The day of my last interview has arrived!

We visit another beautiful town in Japan called Nara, with its gorgeous temples covered in snow, and deer walk around freely, come up to us, sniff, and gently nudge our elbows if we are eating a snack. Three temples here are UNESCO heritage sites: the Kofuku-ji temple, with its five-story pagoda and its Eastern Golden hall containing several beautiful statues; the Todaji temple, which houses the largest bronze Buddha in the world as well the largest wooden structure in the world; and the Shinto Kasuga Grand Shrine, which we reach by following a path in a forest and passing around 3,000 stone or bronze lanterns donated by common people as tokens of faith and thankfulness. The path is lined with food stands, where salespeople are getting ready to produce large quantities of doughnuts, shish kebabs, fried or boiled sweet potatoes, a kind of a large wafer on which they squirt some mayonnaise and place a sunny-side up egg, and other foods. Hordes of Japanese visit the temples on 31 December as well as on 1 January. They throw coins to different gods and ask for blessings for the family.

We end our little excursion by eating "*nabe,*" a typical Japanese winter dish, in a restaurant. A small gas stove is placed on the table with a large pot of boiling bouillon. On another plate are vegetables, different types of meat, fish, or tofu, which you dip in the boiling bouillon. When it's ready, you ladle the meat, the bouillon, and the vegetables into a little bowl, eat the food with chopsticks, and drink the soup with a wide, wooden spoon. It is perfect after having walked around in the cold.

At 7 p.m. we are back in the apartment, and I still have not interviewed anybody. Skype seems to be the only answer. Who to pick? I want the interview to be really special.

As a kid, I lived temporarily with some wonderful neighbors. Thirty years have passed since then but our bond is still very strong. AnneMa and Kare are now 89 years old but still live in that same house where I grew up. Maybe they are home? I call them.

"Hallo!" It is the same good voice from before. AnneMa tells me that her father, when he was 88 years old, travelled to visit the missionaries in Japan.

"AnneMa, tell me three things that make you happy."

"I think a lot about the fact that in Christianity I am allowed to be God's child. My father, who was a psalm writer, wrote a song about the security it gives to be a child of God. This makes me truly happy.

"I am also so grateful for the fact that I am healthy and can get up every morning." She laughs and adds, "Also that I can live in Norway!

"Another cause for happiness is my relationship to my siblings and my children. We used to be seven children but, as you know, my brother Oluf passed away a few years ago so now we are only six. But we call each other every day. Our childhood was wonderful. We have also been very blessed with our two children, Harald and Marianne, and her five kids. Now we even have two great-grandchildren."

As she speaks a warm feeling rushes through me, and the same security, trust, and love I felt for them as a child return.

"What is your definition of happiness?"

"Isn't that to be in peace with God and the people around you? I am so happy to know that I have a Father in Heaven who loves me, no matter what. I have also had a sweet husband for 55 years."

She is silent for a while, reflecting upon her life.

"You know, Elisabeth, when you reach my age, it's a wonderful thing to be able to look back and be grateful for the good life you have had—and I really have."

"AnneMa, if I gave you one wish, what would that be?"

"I wish that I will preserve my wits about me until I die. I have prayed a lot to God that he will grant me a peaceful and good death. I would like to be able to live at home as long as possible."

"Are you happy?"

"Yes, I must say that I am. I try not to look at what I don't have and rather focus on all what I have received in my life, quite undeserved. I try to look back on a rich and good life that I have been granted. I am happy but sometimes I feel that I could have been a better person. But this is what is so fantastic: God did not come for those who were perfect; he came to the small and imperfect people. The day we got married the priest said to us, 'The Lord is your Guardian. The Lord is your Shadow at your right hand.' I wrote this on our wedding picture."

And with these words, I finish the 365th interview of the year!

With large letters, I write "THE END" on my notepad.

About the Author

Did you ever wonder what really makes people happy? "Ask them!" recommends Elisabeth Oosterhoff. She followed her own advice and embarked on a yearlong happiness journey, collecting 365 interviews from people of all ages across three continents. The result is her book, *The Many Faces of Happiness: Inspiring Stories on What Makes People Happy.*

Born in Sweden and a Norwegian national, Elisabeth grew up in a number of European countries that sparked her love of learning about different people, cultures, and languages. She finally settled in New Jersey with her husband, son, and furry sidekick, Chino, a Cocker Spaniel. When not chatting up strangers (after all, strangers are just friends we haven't met yet), you can find her working at the United Nations in New York City, where she gets to meet people of different cultures every day.

"The year I spent interviewing one person each day about happiness and all the amazing people I met who were willing to share their life experiences," she says, "was one of the happiest years of my life."

Their stories about happiness create a wonderful feeling that Elisabeth wants to share with others.

You can follow Elisabeth at www.manyfacesofhappiness.com and Facebook.com/ManyFacesofHappiness.

Acknowledgments

I have to start by thanking God for giving me the idea of interviewing one person a day for an entire year. It was an extraordinary gift that could only have come from Him!

To all the wonderful people I met along the way, and who shared their stories with me, I thank you from the bottom of my heart. Without you, this book would not have been possible.

Thank you as well to my "creative team." My awesome octogenarian Aunt Marguerite, who diligently read all my interviews (12 piles, one for each month, are now resting on her dining room table in Norway), provided feedback, and cheered me on. I will always cherish the countless hours spent on trans-Atlantic phone calls debating the interviews.

A huge thanks go to my friends Tine Hatlehol and Erika Mendez for helping me write a great bio and introduction, and for always being so supportive. Having you in my corner means a lot to me!

I had originally thought of undertaking all the steps involved in self-publishing by myself. But after meeting Karen Hodges-Miller at one of the classes she teaches on the subject and enjoying her sense of humor and writing skills, I know today that I chose the right publisher. Thank you for your patience, hard work, and our shared moments of laughter.

It was through her that I met the talented designer Eric Labacz, whose flowery cover I fell in love with as soon as I lay my eyes on it! Thank you!

Sometimes in life we get unexpected lovely gifts: Apart from her fascinating interview, Karen Mintz created my website www.manyfacesofhappiness.com. For this I thank her but, even more importantly, for our friendship. She is a wonderful film producer. I invite you to check out her site at www.karenmintz.com.

My friend Eskinder Debebe deserves my gratitude for taking such a nice picture of me for this book.

My heartfelt thanks go to Susan Torres: Thank you for your guidance, your friendship, and for always believing in me. Reading your memoir *Living on Three Spoons* inspired me to follow my dreams of becoming an author, too!

Last, but not least, thank you to my family, colleagues, and friends who have encouraged me to publish this book. A special thanks to my son, Nama, who has always been very supportive of my project, and to my husband, John Peter, who wanted me to promise (I did not agree!) never to undertake such a project again. I love you!

Made in the USA
Middletown, DE
02 March 2020